AFGHANISTAN

The Soviet Invasion in Perspective

HOOVER INTERNATIONAL STUDIES

RICHARD F. STAAR, GENERAL EDITOR, 1978–1982
PETER DUIGNAN, GENERAL EDITOR, 1982–

Publications in the Hoover International Studies series of the Hoover Institution on War, Revolution and Peace are concerned with U.S. involvement in world and regional politics. These studies are intended to represent a contribution to the discussion and debate of major questions of international affairs.

South Africa: War, Revolution, or Peace?, L. H. Gann and Peter Duignan

Two Chinese States, Ramon H. Myers, editor

The Panama Canal Controversy, Paul B. Ryan

The Imperialist Revolutionaries, Hugh Seton-Watson

Soviet Strategy for Nuclear War, Joseph D. Douglass, Jr., and Amoretta M. Hoeber

Science, Technology and China's Drive for Modernization, Richard P. Suttmeier

Waiting for a "Pearl Harbor": Japan Debates Defense, Tetsuya Kataoka

The End of the Tito Era, Slobodan Stankovic

Communist Powers and Sub-Saharan Africa, Thomas H. Henriksen, editor

The United States and the Republic of Korea, Claude A. Buss

The Clouded Lens: Persian Gulf Security and U.S. Policy, 2d ed., James H. Noyes

Communism in Central America and the Caribbean, Robert Wesson, editor

Ideology of a Superpower, R. Judson Mitchell

A. U.S. Foreign Policy for Asia, Ramon H. Myers, editor

The ASEAN States and Regional Security, Sheldon W. Simon

The Struggle Over Eritrea, 1962–1978, Haggai Erlich

Conflict in Northwest Africa: The Western Sahara Dispute, John Damis

Oil Supply Disruptions in the 1980s: An Economic Analysis, Karim Pakravan

The Arabian Peninsula: Zone of Ferment, Robert W. Stookey, editor

The Iron Triangle: A U.S. Security Policy for Northeast Asia, A. James Gregor and Maria Hsia Chang

Greek Politics at a Crossroads: What Kind of Socialism?, Roy C. Macridis

Gulf Security into the 1980s: Perceptual and Strategic Dimensions, Robert G. Darius, John W. Amos, II, and Ralph H. Magnus, editors

Afghanistan: The Soviet Invasion in Perspective, revised ed., Anthony Arnold

AFGHANISTAN

The Soviet Invasion in Perspective

REVISED AND ENLARGED EDITION

ANTHONY ARNOLD

HOOVER INSTITUTION PRESS

Stanford University, Stanford, California

Cover photograph: Photri

Hoover Press Publication 321

Copyright 1985 by the Board of Trustees of the
   Leland Stanford Junior University

Revised Edition, first printing, 1985
First edition, 1981; second printing, 1982
Manufactured in the United States of America
89 88 87 86   9 8 7 6 5 4 3 2

Library of Congress Cataloging in Publication Data

Arnold, Anthony.
   Afghanistan, the Soviet invasion in perspective.

   (Hoover international studies)
   (Hoover Press publication)
   Bibliography: p.
   Includes index.
   1. Afghanistan—History—Soviet occupation,
1979–   2. Afghanistan—Foreign relations
—Soviet Union. 3. Soviet Union—Foreign
relations—Afghanistan. 4. United States—
Foreign relations—Afghanistan. 5. Afghanistan
—Foreign relations—United States. I. Title.
II. Series.
DS371.2.A76   1985   327.470581   85-808
ISBN 0-8179-8212-4

To my friends the Afghans
As in the past,
enshalla,
Your pride, courage, and
individualism
will prevail

Contents

Editor's Foreword
to the Revised Edition

In this revised edition of his book on Afghanistan, Anthony Arnold brings up to date the Soviet invasion and the struggle for that beleaguered country. The Afghans continue to fight bravely, albeit crudely, without sufficient modern weapons, proper training in tactics and command, or adequate communications and transport. Arnold cogently and forcefully traces events in Afghanistan from 1979 to 1984 and he provides clear answers to two fundamental questions: Are the Soviets committed to taking and keeping Afghanistan within the Soviet empire? What are U.S. policy options?

The Soviet position in Afghanistan is not irreversible, according to Arnold. He believes the Soviets have left the door open for a retreat from Afghanistan under certain conditions. The United States, therefore, should not write off the Afghans as lost forever to the Soviet empire. Afghan resistance, though important, will not be the key to Soviet withdrawal; rather, divisions within the Soviet Union and the bloc, and world opinion, will be more important. The Soviets cannot be beaten by the Afghans, but resistance at home to the war plus international pressure may force a Soviet pullout. The costs of the war are great; an end to the struggle would thus bring great economic savings, stop draft resistance, and regain world popularity and respect for a unique pacific act.

U.S. policy should aim to internationalize the Afghan struggle, that is, to gain support for the mujahideen at the U.N., in Paris, London, Bonn, Cairo, and such places. Pressure on the Soviets must be increased worldwide. The Reagan administration has budgeted $280 million for Afghan resistance, and this active support—with arms and money—must continue if Afghanistan is to be liberated. No U.S. forces are required and none should be promised. If U.S. support is firm, Pakistan may prove more helpful to the Afghans than at present. They have to be united and better trained with antitank and antiaircraft missiles to raise the price for the Soviets of staying in Kabul. But we do not wish to create an Afghan client state linked to the West; this would be impossible for the USSR to accept. A free but neutral Afghan nation should be the objective, not only for the Afghan people but also for the West.

Peter Duignan

Coordinator, International Studies Program
Hoover Institution

Editor's Foreword
to the First Edition

From being one of the least known countries in the world, Afghanistan has been catapulted into the world limelight since the Soviet invasion of December 1979. It is premature to assess the full significance of that event, if for no other reason than the fact that its ultimate success remains in doubt. The Afghans, against all odds and logic, go on fighting. USSR troops, after a year of battle, appear no closer to victory than they were at the outset.

It is not too early, however, to observe and comment on the events that led up to the invasion or to point up some of the unique features of the situation that already have become apparent.

In invading Afghanistan, the Soviet Union appeared to be setting a new and more aggressive pattern in its foreign policies. If one compares certain military occupations by Stalin in 1939 and 1940 (eastern Poland, the Baltic states, parts of Finland), one must acknowledge that all of these lands once had belonged, rightly or wrongly, to tsarist Russia. Despite opposition to Soviet rule by the vast majority of their populations, Stalin, as de facto heir to the tsars, could lay claim to at least some historical right to the territories.

Afghanistan, by contrast, had never before been conquered or occupied (except for temporary cross-border bridgeheads) by either tsarist or Soviet troops. The invasion thus represents a precedent of considerable significance, one that seems to presage a willingness by the USSR to project its military power abroad with less constraint than in the past.

That the USSR had decided to do so cannot be explained by any single factor. Though one may argue as to the relative importance each of the following considerations held in Soviet eyes (indeed the relative weight of each probably differed in the minds of principal Kremlin decisionmakers), all undoubtedly played some role:

Changing Correlation of Forces Soviet perceptions of their own military power and growing relative strength vis-à-vis the West clearly represented an important factor. The temptation to experiment with Soviet armed forces directly (rather than via proxies such as the Cuban troops in Africa) must have been strong. One can even speculate that ranking Soviet military officers could have wanted to expose their units to combat conditions as a means of giving them real-life experience obtainable in no other way.

Strategic Importance of Afghanistan Though a poor country, Afghanistan's strategic location—at the gateway to Middle East oil reserves, close to warm water ports, and on the flanks of China and Pakistan—provided both economic and geopolitical incentives for intervention.

Ideological Investment After the 1978 coup, the USSR had an ideological investment in the Kabul regime, an investment that was threatened by mounting domestic Afghan insurrection. Although not technically obligated under the Brezhnev Doctrine to intervene, the USSR clearly would have been embarrassed if noncommunists had overthrown Hafizullah Amin.

One can imagine each of the key Politburo members accepting one or another of the above arguments as the dominant consideration: Brezhnev, the economic and geopolitical aspects; Ustinov, the military; and Suslov, the ideological.

Probably none of these, however, would have justified intervention if it had not been for one final consideration: the almost certain belief that there would be no effective American response to the invasion. United States armed forces were far away from the region, so they could not act as a deterrent. Perhaps even more important was the psychological element, namely, the apparent absence of any readiness to oppose the USSR. If there had been any residual Soviet concern about a possible American reaction, it is likely that it lost all credibility when the United States failed to respond swiftly and resolutely to the taking of American hostages by Iranian students in November, less than eight weeks before the invasion of Afghanistan.

Nevertheless, in the year that has elapsed, the effects of the invasion itself have been to reverse the trend toward neo-isolationism in the United States. National defense became a key issue in the 1980 presidential election, there has been renewed American recognition of Soviet expansionist ambitions, and there is stronger resolve to oppose them. Some of the specific costs to the USSR probably were foreseen in the Kremlin: the embargo on grain and advanced technology, the failure of SALT II to pass the Senate, and the curtailment of the scientific exchange program. Others perhaps were not anticipated: the Olympic boycott, the strength of the UN General Assembly vote against the USSR (104 to 18), and the augmentation of the effects of the U.S. grain embargo due to poor harvests elsewhere in the world and especially in the USSR itself.

If the above elements continue to work against Soviet interests, that fact perhaps can be attributed more than anything else to the determination of the Afghan population to go on fighting despite the odds. Had the USSR succeeded in a Czechoslovakia-type rapid and bloodless occupation, the chances for sustained Western sanctions would have been much reduced. Instead, the resistance continues to eat away at Soviet strength, prestige, and credibility. As a result, Afghanistan has become a pivotal issue not only for 1980 but perhaps for the decade ahead, with ever-broadening ramifications for the USSR, other Soviet-controlled countries, the West, and all of Asia.

This book examines the events that led to Soviet armed intervention. The progression from economic to political to military interference in order to establish Soviet control is not limited to Afghanistan. Perhaps an early identification of similar techniques employed elsewhere by the USSR may also lead to timely deterrence against future Soviet resort to military force.

Richard F. Staar

Director of International Studies
Hoover Institution
October 31, 1980

Preface

Since the death of Stalin, serious students of the USSR in the United States have tended to gravitate toward one of two distinct views of that country.

One view (Group A) sees the USSR as essentially just another great power, a rival of course, and one that is aggressive at times, but one that has an underlying set of values roughly equivalent to our own. This group believes that the USSR is really little more than the continuation of the old tsarist empire, with limited and generally legitimate aspirations: strategic survival, economic improvement, expansion of influence, acquisition (perhaps even monopoly) of markets, and increased prestige.

Group A has traditionally included the more dovish of our foreign policy experts, those who have believed through the years that the USSR was maturing, that it would accept strategic parity with the United States as an adequate goal, and that meaningful negotiation with the USSR required only immense patience and the ability to understand and appreciate Russian strategic concerns. In the past there has been a measure of cool complacency in this view of our relations with the USSR.

The Group B view, on the other hand, has tended to accept at face value the implacable hostility of Soviet propaganda, most notably the ideological convictions that history has decreed a violent demise for capitalism at the hands of communism and that it is the duty of the

USSR to assist in that process. This group sees very little real distinction between the meaning of cold war, peaceful coexistence, and détente, with the first of these remaining the most accurate and expressive term. Regarding the possibility of Soviet acceptance of parity, Group B believes that Lenin decided the question long ago in just two words: *Kto kogo?* ("Who [conquers] whom?"). There is no room for parity in such a formulation, and the Soviet determination to achieve superiority is a foregone conclusion. Group B tends to believe that Soviet aggressive intentions are immutable and have been restrained only by the limitations of Soviet capabilities.

In times of relative stability in U.S.-USSR relations, the Group A view is traditionally the more acceptable, if for no other reason than that it is not alarmist. In past times of crisis, such as the Hungarian Revolution (1956), the Cuban missile crisis (1962), and the Soviet invasion of Czechoslovakia (1968), popular outrage swelled Group B ranks in the West temporarily, only to have them dissipate after a short time as the public returned to domestic concerns. As tensions relaxed, the Group A "defensive" interpretation of Soviet moves (designed to deny the evolution of Hungary and Czechoslovakia into platforms for hostile activity against the USSR, or in the case of Cuba, to achieve parity with the United States in the stationing of strategic weapons close to the adversary's territory) would gradually gain ground.

In the case of the 1979 invasion of Afghanistan, however, there was little room for complacency from either viewpoint.

In straight geopolitical (Group A) terms, the Soviet invasion was an aggressive, strategic thrust with apparently clear-cut military and economic objectives: closer Soviet proximity to the ever more vital Middle East oil supplies, a step toward attainment of a warm-water port, an increased capability for intimidating all countries in the region (including China's friend, Pakistan), and a new link in the Soviet chain of containment being forged around China. As the first Soviet military conquest of territory outside its accepted sphere of influence since World War II, the invasion appears to have set a new precedent for aggression.

Paradoxically, from the Group B viewpoint, the Soviet move does have a defensive, as well as offensive, aspect. As will be seen in Chapter 8, the USSR in late 1979 was not technically obliged by the Brezhnev Doctrine to defend the Kabul regime against the religious resistance that threatened to topple it; by Soviet redefinition, that regime no longer counted as socialist and hence had no ideological claim on Soviet protection. Nevertheless, the Soviet leaders may have felt that such doctrinal fine points might be overlooked by the peoples of Soviet Central Asia who—far closer to Kabul than to Moscow in religion, culture, and language—might see only that, just next door, enthusiastic popular support of Islamic nationalism was on the point of overcoming a self-proclaimed Marxist-Leninist ruling clique.

If that had been allowed to occur, there could have been some danger of ideological infection spreading across the border into the USSR, despite the lack of any known organized resistance waiting to embrace the Afghan example and regardless of a higher standard of living that would tend to secure local loyalty to Moscow. The precedent of successful popular defiance of an avowedly socialist regime was one the Kremlin was not ready to accept. Too many other resistance-minded nationalities, inside the USSR itself as well as in other Warsaw Pact nations, might take heart from the Afghan example.

Another dispute frequently associated with the Group A–Group B controversy centers on the degree to which Moscow can (or even wishes to) control a foreign Communist Party. In absolute terms, of course, there is no such thing as complete control of one group of humans by another, and to that extent the argument is meaningless. There is, however, a considerable difference between norms of political argumentation, persuasion, and dissent that are acceptable in the West and the discipline of party obedience that is demanded of Communists. This aspect is generally understood and accepted when speaking of conditions within any given party, but it is more debatable when speaking of interparty relations.

Group A advocates tend to believe that the Communist Party of the Soviet Union (CPSU) can do little more than proffer friendly advice to "fraternal" parties, possibly augmented by private influence on particular individuals. They point to the success of various parties in breaking away from Soviet control, whether those parties were in opposition (as in Spain), in power in an independent communist state (Yugoslavia), or even in power in a Warsaw Pact country (Romania). Because there is far less effective Soviet domination of foreign parties today than in the past, the implication is that this development is considered acceptable, perhaps even desirable, from the standpoint of Kremlin politics. The relationship between the CPSU and foreign parties is depicted as indeed fraternal, one of mutual (if sometimes guarded) trust, somewhat akin perhaps to the relations between the United States and its NATO allies. Group A would add that even if it were the Soviet desire to impose discipline and control, that goal would not lie within Soviet capabilities.

The Group B outlook on this question is that the Soviet intent is for maximum control over foreign parties whenever an opportunity presents itself. This includes attempts to recruit foreign Communists as direct agents of one of the Soviet intelligence services, with the twin goals of keeping the USSR informed on internal party maneuverings and of affecting local decisions in Moscow's interests. The Soviet effort to achieve maximum control is unremitting, and if their capability to do so has become weaker in recent years, that is less due to rejection of control as an end than rejection of terror as a means. The Soviet attitude is not fraternal—it is at least paternal, and it attempts to be patriarchal.

In analyzing Afghan developments, Group A tends to believe that until the Soviet invasion, events occurred largely without the knowledge, much less the interference, of the USSR. The 1965 formation and early activities of the People's Democratic Party of Afghanistan (PDPA), Daoud's 1973 coup, the 1977 reconciliation of the two antagonistic factions of the PDPA, and the plotting that led to Daoud's overthrow in 1978 are assumed to be purely domestic developments. Group A views the 1979 Soviet invasion as a disturbing aberration, perhaps the result of sudden, spontaneous outrage at the death of a Soviet deputy minister of interior in Afghanistan.

Group B, on the other hand, perceives a long-term pattern of Soviet aggressive intentions in the country, modified by the pressures of other Soviet priorities and concerns, restrained by the limitations of Soviet capabilities, concealed by the fear of strong Western reaction should they become known, but consistent and openly emergent as soon as conditions permitted.

This book addresses that thesis.

Acknowledgments

It was at the suggestion of Dr. Richard F. Staar of the Hoover Institution that I embarked on this book. Without his encouragement and the steady flow of materials that he and his competent aide, Margit Grigory, sent me, it is doubtful that it would ever have seen the light of day.

My thanks also go to Hilja Kukk of the Hoover Library, whose pursuit of documentation on obscure facts and personages was relentless. The rest of the staff of the Hoover Library, along with that of the Social Sciences Library at the University of California at Berkeley, gave unstinting help, as did the librarians at the World Affairs Council in San Francisco. (Why can't the rest of the world be as helpful as librarians?)

Finally, for my wife Ruth, no words are enough. She collected and organized a large part of the material for this book, gave unflagging moral support, and suffered patiently through episodes of anger, all while managing a wildly fluctuating household of transient dependents.

None of the above, of course, bears any responsibility for errors of omission or commission that may have slipped into the work. Any such lapses are mine alone.

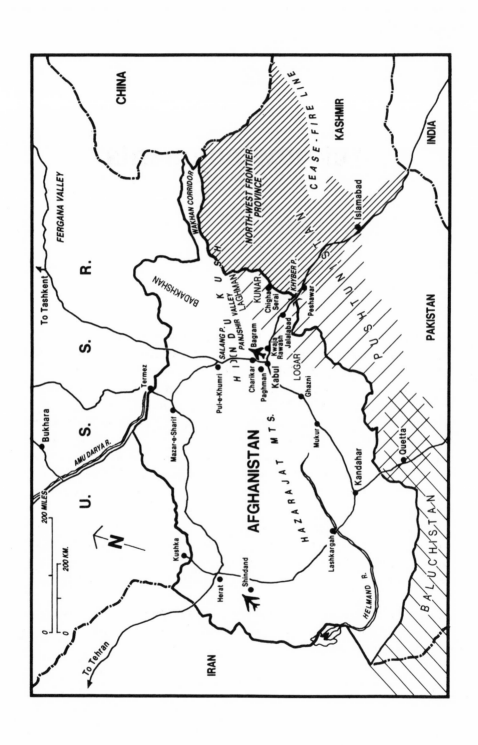

CHAPTER

1

The Historical Setting

The policy and practice of the Russian government has always been to push forward its encroachments as fast and as far as the apathy or want of firmness of other governments would allow it to go; but always to stop and retire when it was met with decided resistance and then to wait for the next favorable opportunity. . . .

(Lord Palmerston, British Foreign Secretary during the First Anglo-Afghan War, in a later [1853] letter to his eventual successor, Lord Clarendon.)[1]

Where the Indian subcontinent collides with Eurasia, the slow-motion conflict of geologic plates has given birth to the highest mountain chain in the world, the Himalayas. Astride their western end lies Afghanistan, the first opportunity in nearly two thousand miles for unimpaired travel north or south around the mountain barrier. It is a stark land of barren deserts and mountains, one-third the size of Mexico, and home today for about 15,000,000 Muslims, most of whom are engaged in subsistence agriculture.

In earlier centuries its strategic position led to alternate enrichment and devastation, as merchants and armies in turn marched through on their way to other lands. Later, a drying climatic trend, combined with the depredations of Genghis Khan and Tamerlane, caused traders to seek an alternative route to the Orient. The opening of the sea lanes in the sixteenth and seventeenth centuries largely destroyed Afghanistan's importance as a commercial crossroads. Its significance as a potential route for military invasion, however, remained unchanged.

In the nineteenth century, the British were keenly aware of tsarist Russia's expansion into Central Asia and of the eventual menace that such expansion might hold for India. Twice during that century the British invaded Afghanistan to forestall what they perceived as a Russian threat to take over the country and to use it as a staging area for an attack on India. Twice the Afghans made it so uncomfortable for them that, within a few years, the British withdrew. The Russians, witnessing this process and perhaps recalling that their own efforts to pacify mountain Muslims in the Caucasus had taken a full sixty-five years, prudently stayed away.

By the end of the century Russia and Britain had reached agreement: the British would control Afghanistan's foreign policy but would not occupy the country or try to manage its internal affairs; Russia formally conceded that Afghanistan lay outside its sphere of influence; and Afghanistan, perforce accepting British control over its foreign relations, dedicated itself to preserving its internal autonomy.

In 1900 Abdur Rahman Khan, the "Iron Amir," who ruled Afghanistan from 1880 to 1901, described his country's vulnerable position: "How can a small power like Afghanistan which is like a goat between two lions or a grain of wheat between two strong millstones of the grinding mill, stand in the way of the two stones without being ground to dust?"[2]

Even before putting the question, Abdur Rahman had found the answer. The solution was to keep Afghanistan from becoming a goat, a grain of wheat, or anything else remotely digestible by the hungriest of imperial lions or the most relentless of imperial millstones. His policies, like those of his predecessors and successors in Kabul's royal palace, were aimed at securing an internal toughness, impermeability, and integrity that would deter any foreign power from undertaking adventures on Afghan soil. At the same time he maintained a capability for smooth maneuvering between potential invaders, balancing one against the other. With these attributes, the Afghan tribes must have seemed to the two imperial millstones more like ball bearings than grains of wheat.

In the end, Russia and Britain came to understand that there were some advantages for all concerned in this situation—at least in the short run. Each had some fear of the other's intentions, and each perceived the useful role an independent country could play in keeping the two empires from coming into inadvertent conflict along a common border. Afghanistan became, in short, a model buffer state. So ideal was it for this role that in 1895 Britain and Russia agreed between them to add to it a new piece of territory, the Wakhan Corridor, running from the main body of Afghanistan to the Chinese border and dividing the North West Frontier Province (NWFP) of India from the Pamir Mountains in Russia. Abdur Rahman, who had to deal with some twenty major tribal insurrections within his own country during his twenty-one-year reign, had no desire to take on responsibility for this whole new set of independent potential insurgents, but he had little say in the matter.[3] He, better than anyone, understood the limitations that his country's economic backwardness had imposed on its independence in international affairs.

At the same time, that very backwardness was vital to continued Afghan internal self-determination. As long as the country remained poor and inaccessible, it would be unattractive to those with imperial designs.[4] The fastest way to build a modern military deterrent against foreign encroachment would be to develop the nation's economy with the aid of foreign investment, but to take that course would be to invite the enslavement it was designed to forestall.

To identify the problem was not to solve it; but in Abdur Rahman's view there was no question as to priorities: national independence took precedence over all other considerations, with unification of the warring tribes that made up the country taking a close second. Only after these two goals had been secured would he be willing to tolerate the foreign involvement necessary for economic development.

He was particularly adamant in his opposition to any kind of railroad construction in the country. Once a railroad was built, he noted, foreign troops could be called in at any time to protect foreign investments or, indeed, merely at the whim of any great power neighbor, and Afghanistan's primitive military forces would be helpless to stop them. Afghan independence would be the inevitable victim.[5] So trenchant were Abdur Rahman's arguments that to this day there are no railroads in Afghanistan, despite periodic proposals for building them. The old amir's pessimism became bitter reality anyway, however: it was the twentieth century equivalents of foreign-built railroads—airports and highways—that literally paved the way for the 1979 Soviet invasion.

With the death of Abdur Rahman in 1901 and the accession to the throne of his son, Habibullah, the former's rigid policies were relaxed to some degree. Habibullah had a lively curiosity, and, among other innovations, he helped introduce the automobile, photography, and hydroelectric power to Afghanistan.[6] He also permitted far more domestic freedom than had his iron-willed father. Specifically, he permitted émigrés whom Abdur Rahman had exiled to return to Afghanistan and to become politically active.

Habibullah reigned in an age when pan-Islamism was spreading, and the phenomenon found reflection in his own court. There were three basic factions, all of them anti-British and pro-Turkish in their sympathies: (1) the conservative-clericals, who saw in Turkey a state that was grappling successfully with the necessary evil of moderniza-tion while still retaining Islam as the anchoring foundation; (2) the moderates, who viewed with favor Turkish modernization (especially the carefully paced nature of that modernization); and (3) the mod-ernist-nationalists, the most anti-British, pro-Turkish of the three, who saw in the Turkish reforms changes that might be introduced in Afghanistan, but at a much faster pace than in Turkey, once their feasibility had been demonstrated.[7] The modernist-nationalist news-paper, *Seraj al Akbar*, kept up a drum fire of anti-British propaganda that drew occasional royal reprimands when it overstepped what the amir felt were safe bounds.

Thus, with the outbreak of World War I, there was considerable pressure on Habibullah to join the Central Powers in their war with Britain and Russia. The amir, however, was well aware of both the geographic distance between Afghanistan and the Central Powers and the immediacy of his British and Russian borders. Consequently, despite agitation by the modernist-nationalists for a *jihad* (holy war) against the British, he maintained a careful neutrality throughout the war.[8] Habibullah was no Anglophile, but he had to reckon with the possibility of a joint Anglo-Russian attack on his country, and he could not afford to be at war with either one of those powers, let alone both at once. He was supported, if tepidly, in this realistic policy by some of the more influential moderates and conservative-clericals.

Even after one of the imperial threats had been removed by the disintegration of Russia into revolutionary chaos, Afghanistan re-mained neutral; the outcome of the war was beginning to become evident, and Habibullah prudently held to his previous policy.

In pursuing a course of relatively benevolent neutrality toward Britain, he was following in the footsteps of an illustrious forebear, Dost Mohammed, who refrained from helping Indian insurgents dur-ing the 1857 mutiny, despite heavy pressure from his countrymen to avenge the British victory over Afghanistan in the First Anglo-Afghan War, some fifteen years before. As a prelude to that war, the British had annexed Peshawar and the surrounding territory that was inhabited by Pashtun tribes ethnically associated with the ruling Pashtuns of Afghanistan. Later, in 1893, the British were to fix their permanent Northwest Frontier Province (NWFP) border with Afghanistan along an arbitrary boundary called the Durand Line, which left the annexed territories permanently outside Afghan control.

Once World War I hostilities were over, Habibullah tried to capitalize on his restraint by asking the British to return voluntarily the Pashtun territories that they had annexed. Like Dost Mohammed before him, Habibullah met with a firm rebuff by the British, who also turned a deaf ear to his demands for Afghan independence in conducting the country's foreign affairs.

Shortly thereafter, on the first night of a hunting trip near Jalalabad in February 1919, Habibullah was killed by an assassin whose sponsor has never been clearly identified. It is not at all unlikely, however, that his son and successor, Amanullah, was connected in some way with his demise.

The evidence for such a conclusion is only circumstantial, but it is consistent. Amanullah had the twin motives of achieving power and, in line with his clearly modernist-nationalist sympathies, of removing power from a father whom he regarded as pro-British. The swiftness with which he took power immediately on his father's death (neatly thwarting an uncle who tried to pre-empt the throne) bespeaks prior planning. The investigation of the assassination, which by all logic should have been pushed with great vigor, lasted just long enough to ensure that all of Amanullah's rivals remained in jail until he had secured firm control of the country. Those who survived this ordeal were then declared innocent and released, whereupon the investigation faded away.

In 1978 there appeared in the communist press hitherto unpublished material that adds even further weight to suspicions against Amanullah. In an article covering Habibullah's last months in power, it is stated that, shortly before Habibullah's assassination, one Taj Mohammed Paghman had fired a pistol at him and missed. Spared because of apparently perjured or confused testimony by two eyewitnesses, Taj Mohammed then wrote death-threat notes to Habibullah, to Habibullah's brother Inayatullah, to the foreign minister, and to the court chamberlain. The handwriting having been identified, Habibullah ordered the execution of Taj Mohammed and several accomplices, including a certain Abdur Rahman Ludin. That same night, however, Habibullah himself was assassinated. The death sentences of Taj Mohammed and the other earlier conspirators were quietly lifted. Only ten years later, after Amanullah himself had been deposed, did his successor have Ludin shot by a firing squad and Taj Mohammed blown from a cannon (the traditional Afghan punishment for especially serious crimes). Ludin and Taj Mohammed are cited in this 1978 communist account as having been "constitutionalists" who were very close to and "worked hand-in-glove with" Amanullah.[9]

Whether or not the circumstantial evidence against Amanullah reflects his direct responsibility for the assassination of his father, one must ask whether there was any foreign involvement in plotting the act. Two isolated pieces of information seem to support that thesis.

The first is a biographic note on Abdur Rahman Ludin (written, incidentally, by a different communist author from the one who described his complicity in the anti-Habibullah plot), in which he is described as "a daring Leftist . . . Especially after he returned from the Soviet Union, where he met Soviet leaders on Revolution Day, he used to praise the Soviets."[10] This trip to the USSR took place in November 1918, less than three months before Habibullah's assassination. While he was there, did Ludin discuss assassination plans with his Soviet contacts? Given the Soviet policy of world revolution at that time, it is difficult to imagine that he (or the Soviets for that matter) would have passed up the chance for such discussions, assuming that Habibullah's removal was already being contemplated by one side or the other.

The second piece of information is a curious statement made some years later by Fedor F. Raskolnikov, Lenin's envoy to Kabul during the early 1920s. Writing in the British journal *Labour Monthly* in 1929, Raskolnikov averred that Habibullah had failed "to take into consideration the changes which World War I and the October Revolution had brought about in the international position of Afghanistan . . . After the October Revolution the Soviet Union was practically at war with Great Britain [but] Habibullah did not understand how to exploit these differences in favor of the national interests of his country and *for this incompetency he paid with his life*."[11] (Italics added.)

In other words, Habibullah was murdered for not waging a war that would be mutually advantageous to Afghanistan (to gain full independence from Britain) and to the USSR (to tie down the British forces, with which the USSR was "practically at war"). The fact of Afghan-Soviet collusion in Habibullah's murder may not be definitely established, but the motive and the instrument (Ludin) lend themselves to that interpretation.

CHAPTER

2

The First Twenty Years
1919–1939

The October Revolution not only changed fundamentally the fabric of domestic life in what had been tsarist Russia, but also involved the new Soviet state in a series of foreign confrontations. In Afghanistan during the same era, Amanullah's accession to the throne resulted in similar domestic upheaval and foreign complications, derivatives of his own experimentation in too-rapid reform at home and risky initiatives abroad. In the end, unlike Lenin and Stalin, Amanullah failed: Afghan traditional patterns proved too strong for his reformist ambitions, absolute ruler though he was. In the meantime, however, Afghan-Soviet relations developed in an intriguing blend of unacknowledged cooperation and hidden betrayal, much of which, even today, can only be inferred.

In late March 1919, just over a month after Habibullah's assassination, the government of Afghanistan received an official communication from the Soviet government, in which it was noted that the Russian Soviet Federated Socialist Republic (RSFSR) would be sending an envoy, one N. Bravin, to Afghanistan and Persia by way of Tashkent. The letter further noted that the RSFSR had annulled all treaties signed by the tsarist government with the rulers of that "global beast of prey," England.[1]

By May 14, when Amanullah's new foreign minister, Mahmud Tarzi, answered the Soviet letter, Afghanistan had attacked India and the Third Anglo-Afghan War was in full swing. In his reply, Tarzi wrote that he would welcome Bravin, but unfortunately the British were bombing Afghanistan "in answer to our establishing good relations with our neighbors." Tarzi also noted that Amanullah, on his first day on the throne, had annulled all of his predecessors' treaties with Britain and had declared Afghanistan's complete independence.[2]

In the meantime, Amanullah himself had written two warm letters to his "great and good friend," Lenin. In the first, dated April 7, he noted in straightforward prose that until then Afghanistan had not had the chance to maintain relations with other nations that "also favor freedom and equality." Inasmuch as Lenin himself had come out in favor of such principles, Amanullah was "happy to be the first to send a friendly word from the Afghan people."[3]

Amanullah's second letter to Lenin was written two weeks later, on April 21. There is no apparent reason for the communication, which appears to consist only of vague platitudes. Perhaps, in the meantime, there had been some other word from Lenin that provided concrete reference points that Amanullah chose to answer in nonspecific terms. Among the more intriguing formulations is his reference to "mutual human relations for removing human poverty [being] a natural demand of mankind, especially in the present century, when the benefits of civilization, bringing happiness, call people to unification [*sic*— soyedineniye*] and friendly mutual relations . . . first among two neighbors and then other peoples."[4] Leaving aside the possibility of hidden meanings in this message, its tone, like that of the earlier message, indicated that relations between Afghanistan and the RSFSR indeed commenced on a warm basis.

According to Raskolnikov, the Soviet Union was practically at war with Britain at the time of Habibullah's assassination. Within three months of that event, Afghanistan was actually at war with Britain—a war that Afghanistan itself precipitated.

Not satisfied with waiting for a decisive British response to his declaration of independence, Amanullah sent his troops down through the Khyber Pass against the opposing British forces on the plains below. Though caught off balance, the British easily defeated the Afghans in the field. Having suffered losses in World War I, however, and with no desire for another debilitating occupation like those of the nineteenth century, the British accepted an Afghan bid for a truce and opened negotiations that eventually led to full independence for Afghanistan.

What led Amanullah to attack Britain, the most advanced military power of the age, a victor in the most destructive war in centuries, a country infinitely richer and stronger than his own? Was it merely an astute reading of the British mood? Or did he have reason to feel he could count on Soviet aid if the British were to counterattack with an invasion of his kingdom? Was he perhaps counting on Soviet support for his claims to the NWFP and the regional capital of Peshawar? If so, he must have been disappointed, for the Soviets, hard-pressed in their own civil war, could offer no aid, and Amanullah had to accept reconfirmation of the Durand Line as the border between his country and India.

Although there is no available record of any Soviet military commitment to Afghanistan in 1919, Amanullah may have been confident at least of Soviet financial backing. Since the days of Abdur Rahman, the British had provided an annual subsidy of more than one million rupees for the Afghan economy. By opening hostilities, Amanullah cut himself off from this support. A year after independence, however, in a treaty signed on September 13, 1920, in Kabul, the USSR obligated itself to supply one million gold rubles annually to the Afghans.[5] In addition, the USSR promised to deliver several aircraft, to provide five thousand rifles and ammunition for them, and to help Afghanistan in establishing an aviation school and a gunpowder plant. Agreement was also reached on sending Soviet technicians and other specialists to Afghanistan.[6] This treaty was not ratified until the following year and in fact was not honored in terms of actual payment until 1924.[7]

Whether or not the USSR specifically prompted the Afghans to undertake their war of independence, the conflict appeared to serve Moscow's interests. It occupied at least some of Britain's military energies and it inspired Indian revolutionaries and other restless colonial dissidents. With the communist optimism of 1919, some in the Kremlin may well have seen in Kabul's victory the harbinger of a whole series of revolts that would sweep through Asia, ending imperial Europe's domination of that continent.

In one respect this judgment was almost correct, but events did not occur as foreseen by Moscow. The most enthusiastic opponents of European imperialism turned out to be not those southern and eastern Asians under British, French, or Dutch rule, but Russia's own Central Asian dependencies adjacent to Afghanistan.

Despite the initial warmth of Soviet-Afghan communications and the eventual aid, the beginnings of disagreement between them in Central Asia were visible from the outset of their relations. The March 27, 1919, letter announcing the dispatch of Bravin to Kabul, for example, was signed by one Bogoyavlenskiy, "People's Commissar of Foreign Affairs of the Turkestan Soviet Republic."

Afghan foreign minister Tarzi's reply, responding point by point in a most friendly fashion to everything written by Bogoyavlenskiy, was not sent to Bogoyavlenskiy at all but rather to Soviet commissar of foreign affairs Georgiy Vasilyevich Chicherin in Moscow. Furthermore, in one cleverly worded sentence, Tarzi staked out an implicit Afghan claim to Turkestan, Bogoyavlenskiy's own purported nation.

"In accordance with a royal decree," Tarzi wrote, "the Governor General of Turkestan has been instructed to receive the Ambassador of the great government of Russia in the best manner . . . and to offer him cooperation and assistance in getting to Kabul."[8]

Tarzi neither identified the governor general nor did he bother to specify whether the Afghan concept of Turkestan included all of the former Russian province under that name. In fact, there is no reason to believe that Kabul actually controlled any significant part of the province. History does not describe Moscow's initial reaction to this paper conquest, but within months Soviet concern began to be expressed privately. In September 1919, Leon Trotsky, Soviet commissar of war, wrote to the Central Committee of the CPSU to warn against an English-sponsored confederation of Persia, Bukhara, Khiva, and Afghanistan, directed against Soviet Turkestan. Whether this was a real or imagined threat, Afghanistan was unquestionably active in helping the emir of Bukhara and the khan of Khiva (both of whom— like the amir of Afghanistan in his relations with the British before 1919—had enjoyed, under the tsars, sovereignty in internal but not in foreign affairs) to defend themselves against the Red Army and to suppress indigenous revolutionaries.[9]

What the Afghans had in mind was the formation of a Central Asian confederation, with Kabul the dominant power. Such a confederation would have provided an excellent buffer against Russian encroachments from the north, as well as furthering Afghanistan's own pan-Islamic aspirations. As a start, Amanullah opened diplomatic relations with Bukhara and Khiva in order to afford them legal recognition as sovereign states. He hoped, ultimately, to do the same with Turkestan, and to include all of them in his projected confederation.[10]

For the Russian Communists, however, the expansion of feudal Afghanistan at the expense of socialist Russia was a historical anachronism: it contradicted not only the proper, programmed course of history as dictated by Marx, but Russian state self-interest as well. The latter half of 1919, however, was a time of serious difficulty for the USSR, as White forces in Russia marched north along the Don River as far as Voronezh, and Moscow itself seemed to be threatened. Whatever the USSR's Central Asian intentions, Soviet capabilities were being critically strained closer to home. It is perhaps for that reason that in November 1919, shortly after Trotsky's warning, Lenin wrote to Amanullah, "Afghanistan is the only independent Muslim state in the world, and fate sends the Afghan people the great historic task of uniting about itself all enslaved Mohammedan peoples and leading them on the road to independence."[11]

If there was any sincerity in these words at all, it lay in Moscow's hope that Afghan pan-Islamic aspirations would find outlets to the east, west, or south—anywhere, in fact, but to the north. It was a vain hope. Afghanistan worked hard to prop up the shaky Bukharan emir and the Khivan khan, and once the Red Army had deposed them (in September 1920), gave them sanctuary and a base from which to operate their governments in exile. Worse, the Afghans gave direct, discreet aid to the Basmachi, partisans who continued to resist Soviet control in the region.

Soviet sources define *Basmach* as "member of a counter-revolutionary band in Central Asia in the period of the struggle to establish Soviet power,"[12] and as deriving from the Turkic word *basmak*, meaning "to fall on, attack."[13] A French scholar asserts that it means "go barefoot" (*va-nu-pieds*),[14] which, whether accurate or not, is evocative of the Basmachi's true status. For they were fundamentally partisans whose common denominator was inferiority in overall numbers and armaments to the Red Army forces they confronted.

Despite the paucity of literature in English on the Basmachi, they are worth closer attention, not so much for their effect on Soviet-Afghan relations (though they were a pivotal factor) as for the striking parallels they provide with today's Afghan insurgent movements. Indeed, it almost seems that the basic difference is only one of area, with the locale having moved south: Afghanistan today is the equivalent of the Central Asian battlefields of yesteryear, while Pakistan is repeating Afghanistan's uneasy former role as a safe haven and undeclared source of support for the insurgency. (Compared with Afghanistan in the 1920s, however, Pakistan is forced to be far more discreet in any aid it might wish to give the rebel cause; the relative strength and proximity of the USSR is far greater.)

Two aspects of the Basmachi movement deserve particular notice. First, it was durable. Regular armed clashes with the Red Army went on for at least fifteen years, from 1917 to 1932, and often involved significant numbers of troops on both sides. For example, Soviet sources (who have no reason to emphasize Basmachi strength) put Basmachi numbers in the Fergana valley alone at thirty thousand during the summer of 1920.[15]

Second, there is a consistent record of betrayal of the Soviet cause by Moscow's own protégés on the spot, and an equally consistent Basmachi record of success in commanding loyalty among the local population, despite the overwhelming odds against them. Corollary to this was the bewildering facility of the lesser Basmachi leaders and their followers to make apparent capitulation to the Red Army, to volunteer service with it, and then to betray it at the first opportune moment.[16]

For some reason, despite Soviet recognition of this pattern and the resultant general order that all capitulating Basmachi be disarmed, dispersed, and held under close control, the Soviets kept falling into the same trap. The Basmachi were such good fighters and so familiar with the terrain that the temptation to use them was irresistible. (In 1980 there were reports of a similar program: Afghan tribesmen from one section of the country were allegedly being hired at ten times the normal soldier's daily wage to fight insurgents in other parts.[17] It is not clear whether such forces were working directly with Soviet troops or alongside regular Afghan units. Either way, frictions, betrayals, and mutinies would seem to be the inevitable result.)

Perhaps the most famous of the Basmachi "traitors" was Enver Pasha, who had been the young war minister of the Ottoman empire during World War I. Having been ousted from that position following defeat of the Central Powers, he went first to Germany and then on to Moscow, where he became known as a nationalist Bolshevik. He persuaded Soviet authorities that he could rally the Central Asian Muslims into an anti-British *jihad*, and using Afghanistan as a base, drive the English from India. With Soviet backing he went off to Bukhara but in November 1921, under cover of a hunting trip, he defected to the Basmachi. In early 1922 he helped rally and unite various Basmachi bands, swiftly building an army of some twenty thousand. And on May 19, 1922, as chief of the "Turkish Central Asian Republic," he sent a note to the Russian Socialist Federated Soviet Republic (RSFSR) demanding recall of all Red Army troops then stationed in Khiva, Bukhara, and Turkestan.[18]

Although Enver Pasha was the most famous, he was by no means the only such defector from the Soviet ranks. The Red Army had taken Bukhara on September 3, 1920,[19] and had set up the appropriate party and state organizations, staffing their upper levels with ideologically "correct" leaders. It was doubtless this apparent control that permitted the USSR, some eleven days later, to agree solemnly by treaty in Kabul that Bukhara and Khiva would be granted complete self-determination.[20] The Afghans, who had insisted on this proviso as one way of gaining prestige with fellow Muslims, were perhaps unaware of the reason for the sudden Soviet acquiescence. Probably by the time their own communications could inform them of the Soviet takeover of the two states, the treaty already had been signed—though not ratified.

Through the next year the Soviet leadership in Bukhara apparently behaved as obediently as Moscow expected. The Afghans, possibly feeling that they had been double-crossed, did not ratify the treaty until August 1921.[21] When they did, it may have been because in this specific instance their information was better than that of the Soviets. It was in that same August that the chief of the Central Executive Committee of the Bukharan People's Soviet Republic, Usman Khodzha Pulatkhodzhayev, turned over to the Basmachi twelve Red Army collaborators, six of whom were summarily executed.[22]

If the Afghans appeared to know of this act and recognize its significance, Moscow clearly was unaware of it; Pulatkhodzhayev remained in power until December 1921 when, in an attempt to disarm by trickery and then to arrest the Red Army garrison at Dushanbe, his true pro-Basmachi allegiance emerged.[23] In the aftermath of this failed effort, the extent of anti-Soviet sentiment among the Bukharan leadership suddenly became clear. How many actually went over to the Basmachi is unrecorded, but they included the commissar of war and his deputy, the chief of police (militia), and even the chief of the secret police (Cheka)![24] (It is an irony of history that the Uzbek Fayzullah Khodzhayev, the only prominent Central Asian leader to remain unshakeably loyal to Moscow through these turbulent years, was to be executed by Stalin in the 1937 purges—as a bourgeois nationalist!)[25]

In fact, it was not a question of these individuals being defectors, any more than the Hungarian leadership under Imre Nagy or the Czech leadership under Alexander Dubcek were defectors. In all three cases, the population supported the so-called renegades in their bid for independence, and it was only the appearance on the scene of an overwhelming alien military force that restored Moscow's control. Even the language used by Soviet propaganda in Central Asia served as a precursor of what was to be repeated three and four decades later in Europe—and nearly sixty years later in Afghanistan. As expressed in a session of the Bukhara soviet in August 1922, after more obedient leaders had filled the seats vacated by Pulatkhodzhayev and the others, "The Russian Red Army came to Bukhara not on its own initiative, for the sake of achieving some mercenary goal, but, on the contrary, at the request of the Bukharan People's Soviet Republic, to liberate its territory and downtrodden people from the ongoing Basmachi Movement."[26]

Soviet actions in Central Asia during this period resulted in popular reactions in Afghanistan itself. In 1919, the Bravin mission lost two killed, and eighteen wounded, in one armed attack. In 1922, five members of the Soviet embassy were killed in Kabul, an unsuccessful attempt was made on the lives of the consul general and other members of his mission in Herat, and several couriers were murdered. A Soviet source ascribes these attacks to the actions of British agents, but without any evidence to support the charge.[27] It is more likely that at least the 1922 attacks were by displaced Basmachi or by Basmachi sympathizers.

Afghan popular opinion in favor of the Basmachi was a key factor in permitting that movement to remain viable for another decade despite Red Army efforts to stamp it out. Afghan sympathy permitted Basmachi bands to cross at will over a border too difficult for the Red Army to patrol effectively, and this was an important factor in their survival. Soviet sources accuse world imperialism of having supplied significant material support to the Basmachi, but the evidence they produce to substantiate this charge indicates a low level of quantity and quality of foreign aid (e.g., occasional interceptions of camel trains with some rifles and ammunition).[28]

Although the USSR did eventually quell the movement, the

nationalism that lay at its roots is an innate (if occasionally dormant) aspect of any particular culture dominated by another. Indeed, with the example that the Afghan insurgency is providing today, it is not impossible that violent manifestations of nationalism will recur in Soviet Central Asia in the not-too-distant future.

The Basmachi movement was to reach a peak in 1922 just before Enver Pasha's death in action (he commanded twenty thousand troops at the time, besides having the allegiance of the former Soviet leadership in Bukhara).[29] By then, however, a series of diplomatic moves was already paving the way for firmer Soviet control over the territory north of Afghanistan.

The Afghan-Soviet treaty signed in 1920 and ratified by Kabul in 1921 contained, in addition to its articles on the various Soviet assistance measures and Khivan/Bukharan "self-determination," provisions for establishing Soviet consulates in five Afghan towns and for reciprocal Afghan privileges in the USSR.[30] This Soviet consular representation was far in excess of any justifiable need, at least as far as normal diplomatic transactions were concerned, and was looked upon with understandable skepticism by the British.

Perhaps as a result of this skepticism, the preamble to the Anglo-Soviet trade agreement signed in March 1921 included a Soviet obligation to refrain from any military or propaganda moves that might affect British interests in India or Afghanistan. This appeared to hold up a Soviet project for dispatching Indian revolutionaries via Afghanistan to India.[31] It did not, however, put a stop to similar activities already under way, and in 1923 the British forced the recall of the Soviet ambassador in Kabul, threatening an economic boycott in retaliation for his aid to Pashtun rebels in the NWFP.[32]

Finally, in November 1921, the Afghans and the British signed their own agreement, containing among other provisions an Afghan pledge not to permit the establishment of Soviet consulates in eastern Afghanistan.[33]

Until this time, Amanullah had been experimenting rather freely in international intrigue. Not only had he lent support to the Basmachi in Soviet Central Asia, but (at least according to Soviet sources) he had closed an eye to British activities in the same field. At the same time, with traditional Afghan evenhandedness in such matters, he had not objected in principle to the passage of men and arms from the Soviet Union through Afghanistan on their way to stir up trouble in India, though he did insist that the two proceed separately, the arms to be under strict Afghan control during passage.[34]

Amanullah was, however, under increasingly heavy economic pressure. The Soviet subsidy at this time was still only a promise and his own internal reforms were proving more expensive than anticipated. Not only were they expensive financially, but they began to incur some unpleasant political costs as well. In 1925 a revolt against his rule broke out in Khost, and it was only put down thanks to the use of German and Soviet pilots flying missions against the rebels.[35]

That same year Soviet forces occupied a small island in the Amu Darya River (known as Urta Taigal or Yangi Qala), on the border with Afghanistan. The Afghans protested, and as a result of the findings of a joint Afghan-Soviet border commission, Afghan possession of the island was confirmed.[36]

It was probably a combination of Soviet "fraternal assistance" against Amanullah's internal enemies and the peaceful acceptance of the border commission's findings that resulted the following year in an outwardly more cordial Soviet-Afghan treaty, one that seemed to rule out any further Afghan support to the Basmachi.[37] In fact, however, there was very little change; the Afghans were to plead, and the Soviets to agree, that there was little of a practical nature the Afghans could do to deny their territory to the Basmachi.[38]

At the same time, the Afghan tilt toward the USSR may also have been partially responsible for a greater Soviet aggressiveness in 1926–27 as the USSR tried to stir up trouble in British-controlled Baluchistan, to the south of Afghanistan. Like the previous attempt among the Pashtuns, however, the attempt was frustrated by British threats of economic retaliation.[39]

While backing away from these efforts at subverting India, the USSR continued to increase its influence inside Afghanistan. The thirteen Soviet aircraft that had helped to put down the Khost revolt remained as a gift to the Afghans, along with the loan of thirty pilots to operate them. Soviet engineers began work on a road to connect Kabul to the northern provinces, and Soviet nationals began to appear ever more frequently in Afghan government offices.[40] In small measure the USSR was attempting then what it was to repeat on a much grander scale thirty years later.

Meantime, however, the world was moving toward the pivotal year 1929, memorable in the West for the onset of the Great Depression, in the USSR for industrialization/collectivization, and in Afghanistan for the temporary dispossession of the monarchy by a Tadzhik bandit, Bacha-e-Saqao ("waterboy's son").

The fall of Amanullah in Afghanistan was the direct result of his unpopular reforms. Among other gestures disruptive of the status quo, Amanullah decreed that Afghan males should wear Western dress when in Kabul. He also demanded land reform, women's education, and abolition of the veil for women. These reforms, supposed to set the country on the road to modernization, produced a backlash of surprising ferocity that led instead to a temporary breakup of the Afghan state. The tribes rose up in rebellion, warring first against Amanullah and then—as has been traditional throughout Afghan history when central power has been eliminated—against each other. Bacha-e-Saqao took over Kabul and with it the ostensible reins of power. He did it, however, with a robber band that was no substitute for the semi-professional Afghan army and with a set of "ministers" most of whom were illiterate. He lasted for nine months, only to be over-thrown and executed by Nader Shah in late 1929.

Nader Shah had returned to Afghanistan with tacit British aid, accompanied by his two brothers and raising an army of Pashtuns as he passed through the NWFP. (He was specifically enjoined from doing this by the British, perhaps because they thought he might overlook the opportunity if they did not remind him of it; there was no doubt in anyone's mind that the only sensible way to go about restoring a responsible monarch to the throne was by application of adequate military force.)

Before Nader Shah and his brothers fought the decisive battles that disposed of Bacha-e-Saqao, a similar incursion from the north under Soviet auspices had met with failure. Ghulam Nabi, Afghan ambassa-dor to Moscow, appeared on the Soviet-Afghan border at Termez with some eight hundred "Afghan volunteers" who inexplicably material-ized on Soviet territory with machine guns, artillery, and even air support. His purpose, said Ghulam Nabi, was to restore Amanullah to the throne. To aid Ghulam Nabi in managing his "Afghan" forces came a Russian, one Primakov, a former Soviet military attaché in Kabul. After some initial successes, including the conquest of Mazar-e-Sharif and the recruitment of a motley (but now truly Afghan) troop of volunteers to augment his Soviet contingent, Ghulam Nabi withdrew to the north. He had learned that Amanullah, then in Kandahar and sensing the dissolution of his remaining support in the country, had decided to remove himself to India and to give up the fight.[41]

It had been a curious invasion for several reasons. The concept was probably to have Ghulam Nabi march on Kabul at the head of the same army whose hard corps was Primakov's disciplined, thinly disguised Soviet unit. After restoring Amanullah, Ghulam Nabi would have been the power behind the throne, while Primakov (presumably) would have been the power behind Ghulam Nabi. At that point, the USSR would have had an excellent opportunity to influence if not largely to control the Afghan government.

One might have anticipated that Ghulam Nabi, on hearing of Amanullah's capitulation, would have sent him an urgent appeal to hold fast (or even to come join his northern forces), in anticipation of the final, triumphant drive to the capital. Even if there had been temporary setbacks at the hands of Bacha-e-Saqao's ragged army, surely the infusion of a few more Soviet troops, properly disguised as Afghans, would have turned the tide. But Ghulam Nabi made no such appeal and quietly went into temporary exile in the USSR. Nader Shah then seized the initiative, and although the British did not supply their own military commanders to help him, the new Afghan ruler's implicit debt of gratitude was, if anything, to England, not to the USSR.

At first glance, the support the USSR gave Amanullah (however reformist his intentions) seems out of character. Indeed, it must have been an ideologically painful decision for the Soviet leadership to make. Bacha-e-Saqao was a charismatic peasant leader, Amanullah a hereditary feudal monarch. Soviet support for the latter was difficult to explain to the foreign idealists who made up so much of the USSR's support abroad. Furthermore, from a practical standpoint Bacha-e-Saqao was already in power and would have been much easier for the USSR to champion than to overthrow. Finally, when the USSR did opt for support of Amanullah it did so in such a hesitant, ineffective way that it lost more than it would have if it had done nothing at all. Why did it move in the direction it did, and why with such uncharacteristic indecisiveness?

As to direction, it may be that the USSR detected in the charismatic Tadzhik peasant a much greater potential menace to its own restless Central Asian republics than the Pashtun king, Amanullah. The former had direct ethnic ties with the rebellious Tadzhiks who made up so much of the Basmachi movement, and he could be expected to expand his influence northward. Fresh in the Russian memory were the betrayals of the entire Bukharan Soviet leadership when Moscow had tried to exert control before. There was, if anything, less reason for the USSR to put its trust in the self-made Bacha-e-Saqao than it had in Pulatkhodzhayev, its own protégé. By contrast, Amanullah's interests and ties lay in the equally restless Pashtun tribes that were causing the British such problems in the NWFP.

The hesitancy of the Soviet approach was probably caused by Moscow's dawning perception of a domestic problem: the massive peasant discontent with agricultural collectivization throughout the USSR. Peasant resistance was solidifying everywhere and was accompanied in Central Asia by a sudden resurgence of the Basmachi phenomenon.[42] This was no time for Soviet commitments to be extended or for Soviet armed forces to be occupied anywhere but in the homeland, where they were needed to suppress internal unrest.

For his part, Nader Shah, correctly gauging his countrymen's implacable hostility to the reforms imposed by Amanullah, backed quickly away from the most radical of them. The fragility of the Afghan nation-state had been clearly illustrated by its fragmentation when Amanullah was deposed, and Nader Shah had as his first order of business the reunification and proper internal administration of his country. To accomplish this, he needed to reduce to a minimum the distractions of foreign affairs and to ensure tranquillity on his borders.

In 1931 Nader Shah signed a new pact with the USSR, one that reiterated and strengthened Amanullah's 1926 commitments against the use of Afghan territory as a base for subversive activities aimed against the USSR (i.e., a safe haven for the Basmachi). Unlike Amanullah, he enforced it. Under the combined blows of the Red Army in Central Asia and the suddenly effective Afghan border patrols, Basmachi activities began to wither. In early 1931, Afghan forces drove Ibrahim Beg, the most durable of the Basmachi leaders, back over the border into the USSR, where he was finally betrayed by a Central Asian tribesman, taken into custody by Soviet forces, and executed after a show trial. By the end of 1931 Basmachi operations running out of Afghanistan had all but ceased, even though Iran-based bands continued to harass Soviet authorities. The last reported cohesive Basmachi raid returned to its Iranian base in 1933.[43]

At the same time, Nader Shah tried to put a stop to anti-British revolutionary activity based in Afghanistan. This effort was exemplified by the Red Shirt Movement, a professedly Leninist Pashtun group that was alternately in and out of favor with Moscow and that tried to stir up trouble in the NWFP. It had enjoyed some covert moral support from Amanullah, but Nader Shah discouraged its activities as much as possible.

Of the two Afghan rulers, Amanullah and Nader Shah, the latter was undoubtedly more effective in permitting the USSR finally to stabilize its uncertain position in Central Asia. Yet to this day, even as it excoriates Nader Shah as a British puppet, Soviet literature regrets the passing of Amanullah from the Afghan political scene. Although Amanullah was progressive in his internal policies, in practical terms he provided more problems to the USSR than did Nader Shah, who was scrupulous in his adherence to traditional Afghan policies of nonalignment and neutrality.

Two particular "anti-Soviet" actions may lie at the root of Soviet displeasure with Nader Shah.

The first was his sweeping dismissal of the Soviet advisors, pilots, and engineers whom Amanullah had invited to help manage the country, while at the same time, he denied a Soviet request for establishment of a commercial mission in Afghanistan. In place of the departing Soviet advisors, he hired Germans, Italians, Japanese, and Indians (but not British).[44] Following the isolationist precepts of Abdur Rahman, Nader Shah wanted as foreign advisors only those who were unlikely to be supported by neighboring armed forces in case of any disagreements.

The second action that displeased Moscow was Nader Shah's forthright disposal of that Soviet favorite, Ghulam Nabi, who by this time had returned to Kabul from his Central Asian exile. Ghulam Nabi's outspoken support for Amanullah did not earn him many friends in the new Nader Shah regime, which also must have looked askance at his former Soviet ties. Eventually, in the fall of 1932, Nader Shah suggested that Ghulam Nabi leave Afghanistan permanently—though with a royal pension on which to maintain himself in appropriate comfort. While pretending to think this over, Ghulam Nabi allegedly started fomenting rebellion "in the southern province," presumably in the restless regions along the Durand Line.[45]

Summoned before Nader Shah in November 1932, he answered the charges against him in an insulting manner and was executed forthwith. (The trial whose verdict condemned him was actually held post mortem.) Although there is no proof that the USSR was directly involved in Ghulam Nabi's purported subversive activities on this occasion, his previous involvement with Primakov and the Soviet irregulars leads to the suspicion that he was not working alone. The south of Afghanistan, then as now, has been an area of considerable Soviet interest, and active Soviet preparations for supporting tribal uprisings in Baluchistan had been proceeding for some time.[46] Furthermore, his boldness in insulting his monarch, an impropriety that turned out to be fatal, may have stemmed from a belief on his part that he had Soviet backing.[47]

Ghulam Nabi's execution ushered in a brief era of political violence that was not to be matched until the communist coup of 1978, nearly fifty years later. In the space of precisely one year, there were five victims in three separate assassination incidents: three members of the British embassy staff in Kabul, the Afghan ambassador to Berlin (a brother of the king), and finally, on the first anniversary of Ghulam Nabi's execution, King Nader Shah himself. In each case the assassin was a student who was studying or had studied at the German School (Nejat) in Kabul.

There is some controversy whether these assassinations were all linked or whether they represented individual acts of terrorism. Running like a common thread through the identified assassins is their previous membership in the Jawanan Afghan (Afghan Youth) movement, the political heir of an earlier organization of the same name whose goal had been formation of a constitutional monarchy. One authority avers that Jawanan Afghan had been driven underground and dispersed when Nader Shah came to power, had fragmented into a myriad of mini-associations, and thus could not have been an organizing force behind the killings.[48]

Others note that Jawanan Afghan retained enough cohesiveness to declare that its aim was the "subversion of the existing government and of its basis, the Islamic code," justifying its revolutionary position on the basis of alleged secret British manipulation of the Afghan government.[49] (This allegation was certainly untrue, but became a consistent major motif in Soviet propaganda on Afghanistan starting in the 1930s.)

In any case, the growth of political opposition inside Afghanistan was most marked in the Nejat, whereas abroad it was concentrated in the Afghan student community in Germany. An important link between these two groups was Mrs. Mehta (Mitha) Singh, the German wife of "a revolutionary Sikh of the Ghadr Party, who, with Moscow's assistance, had taken up residence in Kabul to plot against British rule in India."[50] The Shahi Bazaar Coffee House, which she owned and operated, was a regular meeting place for students from the Nejat school. Mehta Singh himself had acted as a communications link between the students in Kabul and the last surviving member of Ghulam Nabi's family in Germany.[51] Thus, via the Singhs the USSR must have been fully aware of the activities of the rebellious students if, indeed, they were not directly influencing them. The Singhs themselves were closely acquainted with Nader Shah's assassin.[52]

From the standpoint of the Afghan students, however, motivation for the assassinations was probably a blend of local politics and personal revenge. Marxist-Leninist ideology per se does not appear to have played any detectable role, and with the death of Nader Shah the violence abated.

Nader Shah's son and successor, the young Zahir Shah, "reigned but did not rule" for the next thirty years, only coming into his own as a monarch in 1963. In the interim, according to Afghan tradition, his uncles ran the country in his name. A kindly, gentle man, Zahir Shah remained on the throne in all for four decades until he was finally deposed by his forceful first cousin, Mohammed Daoud, in 1973.

For the rest of the 1930s and on into the middle of the 1940s, Afghan-Soviet relations were unremarkable. For the Afghans it was a period of rest and quiet progress, interrupted by some tribal difficulties and other growing pains. For the Soviet Union it was a time of gigantic turmoil: collectivization, famine, the purges, and finally World War II. It is probably thanks to these overriding preoccupations that the USSR backed away from pursuit of more aggressive policies in Afghanistan during this period.

CHAPTER

3

World War II and Its Aftermath

1940–1953

By the middle of 1940, the initial stages of World War II in Europe and the protracted Sino-Japanese War in the Orient appeared to offer implicit sanction for forcible rearrangement of international borders. Following his successful incorporation of the Sudetenland into the Third Reich, Hitler had signed with the USSR a nonaggression treaty that permitted the latter to occupy the Baltic States, Moldavia, eastern Poland, and parts of Finland. Soviet appreciation of these opportunities was expressed not only in propaganda support for Germany against British imperialism, but, more concretely, in trade that supplied food and raw materials to the German economy.

Meanwhile, the Wehrmacht had overrun all opposition on the mainland of Europe, and Britain was the last remaining major opponent confronting Hitler. Virtually all of England's energies were focused on defense of the home island against the cross-channel invasion that seemed imminent.

All of these factors (not least the apparently pro-German bias of the USSR) created a potential opportunity for Afghanistan to reconquer the historically Afghan lands in the NWFP that had been occupied by the British for the last century. Adding to the temptation was an explicit German promise to guarantee Afghan borders up to the limits of the eighteenth-century Afghan Durrani empire (including all of the NWFP and more), as well as the port of Karachi. In return the

Germans asked that the Afghans foment unrest along India's northwest frontiers.[1]

Twice in the past century the Afghans had been given similar opportunities to reconquer their land. In 1857 the Indian Mutiny had all but driven Britain from the subcontinent (and with Afghan help might indeed have succeeded in so doing); and in 1914–1918, the participation of Turkey as a cobelligerent of Germany in World War I had led to efforts to enlist Afghanistan in a *jihad* against Britain. In both of these cases Afghanistan remained true to its treaty obligations with Britain and stayed neutral.

History repeated itself. On August 17, 1940, at a time when Britain's fortunes in the war were at their lowest ebb, Zahir Shah proclaimed Afghan neutrality.

A year later, the Nazi attack on the USSR had changed the USSR from a tacit Axis ally into a blood enemy, and Afghanistan found itself surrounded on three sides by Allied cobelligerents (China, the USSR, and British India) and on the fourth by Allied-dominated Iran. In August 1941, though both Britain and the USSR were still on the defensive and very hard pressed by the Axis, they had acted jointly to eliminate an effort to enlist Iran on the Axis side. Had the Axis effort been successful, it would have secured Iranian oil for Germany and sealed off the USSR's southern flank as a supply route from the West.

Instead, however, on August 25 the USSR and Britain sent forces into Iran and conquered the country, encountering and overcoming only light opposition from the Iranian army and navy. On October 9 and 11, they followed up this military success with diplomatic pressure on Kabul to remove all nondiplomatic Axis personnel from Afghanistan. The charge was that German agitators were fomenting trouble among the Pashtun tribes and causing casualties to loyal native troops along the Indian frontier. These accusations were similar to those made by the British to the Iranian authorities just before the Anglo-Soviet incursion there, and the threat of similar actions against Afghanistan was apparent in Kabul.[2]

The Afghans delayed briefly (by calling for a tribal assembly [*loyah jirgah*] to decide the issue) in honor of the Pashtun code of ethics that obliges a host to provide sanctuary for any guest. In the end they capitulated to Allied pressure, but in an effort to be evenhanded decreed that *all* nondiplomatic persons who were citizens of any of the belligerent powers would have to leave. Furthermore, before proceeding with the deportations, they secured British promises of safe conduct for Axis nationals while they were crossing India en route home. (The British only partially honored this pledge, interning some of the Germans whom they specifically suspected of having carried out subversive activities. The Afghans, though angered by this violation of a solemn commitment, could do nothing in retaliation.)

As World War II widened to include Japan and the United States, Afghanistan began to feel the effects of the conflict on its economy. On the one hand it could sell to the Allies at war-inflated prices all of the surplus foodstuffs it could produce—and move to market. As a result, foreign monetary reserves built up rapidly, especially because there were few goods available to buy from the belligerents. On the other hand, the war completely disrupted those important aspects of the Afghan economy that depended on normal foreign trade patterns. The single largest source of foreign revenues before the war had been the profitable London market for karakul skins. Wartime London had no use for such luxury items, and the beginnings of an American market (which was to develop significantly in the late 1940s) also fell off sharply when the United States became a belligerent in December 1941. The Axis markets were at a complete standstill during the entire war and for some time thereafter.[3]

Another problem caused by the war was the difficulty in replacing manufactured products, especially machinery needed for agriculture, irrigation, food processing, and transportation. The prewar foreign producers of these items were manufacturing armaments, and Afghanistan could not make its own substitutes. Thus the boom in wartime agricultural sales was limited by the inability of the Afghan farmers to bring new land into production, to exploit existing cultivated acreage to the fullest, or to transport harvests to the international markets.[4]

With the end of hostilities, the leadership looked for ways to improve the economy by using its wartime accumulation of foreign exchange. In 1946 it turned to the Morrison-Knudsen Company of Boise, Idaho, for repair and restoration of four irrigation dams, the construction of new irrigation canals, and the rebuilding of 450 kilometers of highway, all in the Helmand Valley, west of Kandahar. The initial contract was for $17 million, which the Afghan treasury was well able to absorb without outside assistance.[5]

As one of the pioneer postwar American efforts to aid an underdeveloped country, the Helmand project suffered from many of the problems and embarrassments that usually beset such efforts: bad cost estimates, cultural conflicts, broken promises, bureaucratic delays, and the like. It is beyond the scope of this work to discuss these in detail. Suffice it to say that the American involvement and presence in the Helmand was to continue for over three decades, and was removed only in late 1978, when insurgency against the newly installed communist government put the lives of Americans there in jeopardy. Its very durability thus bespeaks a considerable measure of success, despite the early difficulties and the complicating political problems discussed below.

Cost overruns soon raised the Helmand project estimate to $40 million, and the Afghans were forced to turn to external financing sources. Loans by the Import-Export Bank amounted to $21 million in 1949 and $18.5 million in 1954; by 1956 Morrison-Knudsen had spent $54 million on the project, and the United States government had become involved as a direct funder of part of the project through the International Cooperation Administration. The loans that the Afghans were able to secure were far smaller than they wished, and the work went forward slowly.[6]

The transition of the project from one that involved a simple contract with a single foreign firm to one that required funding by a foreign bank (and eventually grants from a foreign government) was an unforeseen development. So was the length of time that was to elapse before any positive benefits were obtained. This was in contrast to the Soviet aid projects of the 1950s that gave relatively quick, visible results.[7]

Meanwhile, however, a political problem of long standing became more acute and overshadowed all other foreign policy considerations for Afghanistan. In 1947, with the breakup of British India into the newly independent states of India and Pakistan, the Afghans saw perhaps their last chance to retrieve by negotiation their lost territories in the NWFP. Once the British had departed from the territories, the Afghans would no longer be able to negotiate with those who had originally annexed the disputed area. Pakistan's own rebuff to any Afghan overtures to take back the land was a foregone conclusion. As in previous eras, however, the Afghans were soon disabused of any hopes that the British would reward Afghan restraint in World War II with territorial concessions.

The border (Durand Line) had been established in 1893, when

Indian foreign secretary Sir Mortimer Durand led a delegation to Kabul for talks with Abdur Rahman. The latter had appeared to welcome the fixing of a boundary (even if it did not satisfy Afghan claims) in order to halt what he perceived as relentless British encroachments on his territory. Reference points were agreed upon, with the actual boundary to be determined by survey teams on the spot. These teams were concerned primarily with military offense and defense, but they were supposed also to preserve tribal integrity insofar as possible. Even if the teams had been scrupulously conscientious (which they apparently were not), the Durand Line would have divided an ethnically homogeneous population.

It was particularly galling to Kabul that the 1947 British-run plebiscite in the NWFP to determine which state would have jurisdiction there offered only two choices: India or Pakistan. In Afghan eyes, the choices should at least have included self-determination, if not outright union with Afghanistan. Although 99 percent of those who voted opted for union with Pakistan, only 55.5 percent of the enfranchised electorate turned out to vote. Three political parties championing independence and claiming to represent nearly 50 percent of the electorate ordered their adherents to boycott the plebiscite, on the grounds that the choices were not broad enough.[8] The relatively weak voter turnout indicates that their call was heeded by at least some of the electorate, though many other factors also would have tended to limit the size of the vote in such primitive, rugged territory.

It was this Afghan frustration in pressing their territorial claims that led them to invent the new state of Pashtunistan, comprising not only the NWFP but also the southwest deserts occupied by Baluchi tribesmen. Afghan propaganda endowed this purported nation with a political and social unity that it did not in fact possess: though linguistically and ethnically akin, the various tribes inhabiting Pashtunistan were customarily at war with one another and only occasionally found partial unity when resisting efforts by outsiders to impose foreign control. (It must be noted that the same independent spirit manifests itself on the Afghan side of the border as well: traditionally, rule from Kabul has been no more acceptable to the mountain tribes than rule from Islamabad.)

As a further sign of its displeasure, Afghanistan cast the only vote in the UN General Assembly against admission of Pakistan to the UN in 1947. It later relented and voted to admit its neighbor. But on July 26,

1949, a *loyah jirgah* in Kabul formally and specifically abrogated all of its international treaties that supported the Durand Line as a border or that referred to the status of the Pashtuns.[9]

In the early stages of their campaign to liberate and/or annex Pashtunistan, the Afghans had the support of the Indian government. When as one part of this campaign the Afghans agitated for a new plebiscite that would offer independence as one of the choices, the Indians became less enthusiastic. They had, after all, adopted a policy of firm rebuff to all suggestions that the fate of Kashmir be decided on such a basis. Perhaps as a result, their support for a Pashtun plebiscite waned in the early 1950s.[10]

For the United States, relations with Pakistan and the perceived need to involve that country in one or more pacts aimed at containing the USSR took precedence over other considerations in the region. Regardless of the legitimacy of the Afghan case, the United States could not afford to antagonize the Pakistanis by supporting calls for an independent Pashtunistan.

Support offered by the USSR for Afghan claims during this period was neither enthusiastic nor effective. Having suffered some humiliation in being expelled from Iranian Azerbaidzhan in 1946, the USSR was cautious in its policies in the region. Furthermore, the Afghans had become aware of Soviet operations in the late 1940s involving the infiltration of Central Asian Tadzhik, Uzbek, and Turkomen agents into Afghanistan to contact relatives there for purposes of espionage and subversion. The targets, themselves former Basmachis and refugees from forced collectivization, did not make good subjects for such approaches, and turned in many of these agents.[11] Such operations made the Afghans doubly cautious in seeking Soviet support. (Soviet-Afghan relations, however, were good in other respects: in 1946 the border with the USSR was formally fixed as the center of the main channel of the Amu Darya, and in 1947 there was an agreement to establish a telegraph link between Kabul and Tashkent.[12])

Thus the Afghans found themselves with little international support in pressing their Pashtunistan claims. This did not deter them from making inflammatory propaganda broadcasts in an effort to rouse the Pashtun tribes on the Pakistani side of the border into rebellion, nor did it deter them from infiltrating their own agents into the NWFP. By 1950 these activities had evolved into the dispatch of army irregulars across the border to attack Pakistani outposts, and after one such attack in 1950, the Pakistanis retaliated by unofficially closing their border to Afghan transport: Afghan trucks suddenly became subject to safety inspections and were found to be substandard.[13] Inasmuch as the Afghans were dependent on imports via Pakistan for virtually all products but food, their economy was in danger of coming to a complete halt. The cutoff of gasoline and kerosene supplies was a particularly serious development.

At this point the USSR finally appeared to recognize the opportunity Afghanistan's short-sighted Pashtunistan policy was affording them. On July 17, 1950, a Soviet-Afghan agreement was signed. It provided for an exchange of Afghan agricultural products in return for Soviet petroleum products, cotton cloth, sugar, and other commodities.[14] In addition, the agreement provided for duty-free transit of Afghan goods over Soviet territory.[15]

Although this agreement established the first Soviet-Afghan trade link since the 1930s, it was still essentially only a barter arrangement and did not involve an active Soviet effort at economic penetration. It did cause Afghan trading patterns to change, however, and although the Pakistanis relented within three months of starting their blockade, Afghan international commerce never again reverted entirely to the old channels.

Furthermore, the agreement led the USSR to experiment with applying political leverage on Afghanistan. In the early 1950s, according to one authority, the USSR "offered" to take over from a Swedish company oil exploration in northern Afghanistan.[16] According to another authority, the oil exploration was a UN project to which the USSR raised objections in 1952 because it feared for the security of its industrial complexes in Central Asia. The Afghans appealed quietly to the United States for political support in rebuffing this objection, but they met with refusal.[17]

On this same subject the Soviets were later to confirm that in August 1952 they tendered to the Afghans a formal objection to the presence of "foreign specialists from NATO countries" in northern Afghanistan "in view of the growing striving of western intelligence to gain access and have a free hand" in that area. In reply, the Afghan government stated that NATO specialists would henceforth be barred from the northern regions.[18]

During this period the Afghans also made overtures to the United States for aid in modernizing their armed forces, but without success.

Several factors ruled against such a program. Afghanistan was too remote, and the only convenient land route at that time lay via Pakistan, an American ally but an Afghan enemy because of the Pashtunistan issue. Any arms supply by the United States was bound to complicate even further the delicate relationships that Washington maintained with both India and Pakistan. When Mohammed Daoud became prime minister in 1953 he set aside, temporarily, his personal antipathy for the American ambassador, Angus Ward, and made one final, unsuccessful attempt to secure military assistance. Negotiations again failed, primarily due to the objective factors outlined above but unquestionably complicated by maladroit handling on the American side and excessive touchiness on the part of the Afghans. In a decision of far-reaching consequences, Daoud, furious, turned to the USSR for arms. He never forgave the United States.[19]

Thus it was that Afghanistan was subjected to a series of reinforcing impulses that worked to break down its traditional closed-door policy against its northern neighbor: (1) the isolation and alienation from the West that the Pashtunistan issue had brought about, (2) the initial disappointments and difficulty in financing the Helmand Valley project, and (3) the U.S. rejection of requests first for political support and then for military aid. Despite its traditional suspicions of Russian motives, pragmatic considerations were forcing Afghanistan into a closer accommodation with the USSR.

CHAPTER

4

The Soviet Drive
for Economic Penetration
1953–1963

Like 1929, 1953 was an important turning point for Afghanistan both in terms of local developments and because of events far from its borders. The end of the Korean War saw the United States briefly inclined to look more to its domestic situation than to foreign involvements. By contrast, the death of Stalin in the USSR ushered in an era of more flexible and sophisticated Soviet foreign policy. This development was to affect Afghanistan fundamentally.

For most Afghans, the most important national event of the year was the decision by the ranking members of the ruling family, the Moham-medzais, to entrust management of the Afghan state to the hands of Sardar (Prince) Mohammed Daoud, a first cousin of King Zahir and the commander of the Afghan Army Central Forces garrison. Daoud took office as prime minister on September 20, 1953, and remained in that position for nearly ten years.

Daoud's rise to power marked the end of a tentative three-year experiment (from 1949 to 1952) in political reform by Prime Minister Shah Mahmud. Since 1931 Afghanistan had gone through the motions of periodic parliamentary elections, but the results were traditionally predetermined by the ruling elite in Kabul. Shah Mahmud made no essential change in that process, but in 1949 he did see to it that among those candidates chosen for the Seventh National Assembly there was a significant contingent with a liberal upbringing: of 120 members of parliament, between forty and fifty were dedicated to reform, and these embarked on a program to disrupt traditional patterns of corruption among cabinet ministers.[1]

As the 1952 elections approached, however, the more extreme oppositionists overstepped the bounds of good taste and political prudence by attacking not only the government but also the royal family and even the Muslim religion. Accordingly, the government banned the three opposition newspapers that had been allowed to publish under a law passed by the reform-minded members of parliament, and it arrested the twenty-five most vocal reform leaders. About half of these subsequently agreed to cease antigovernment activities and were released from jail. Some even reached high positions in the government under Daoud.[2] Others did not survive their prison ordeal, while still others were finally released by King Zahir as part of a general amnesty in 1963.[3]

The decision to seek closer relations with the USSR was probably a collegiate one, taken in the highest councils of the Mohammedzais. To implement it and at the same time keep the reins of power in family hands, they had to choose a family member who could work with the Soviets both directly and via his associates. Ideally, such an individual should not be tainted by previous association with Afghan governments that had been cool toward the USSR. At the same time he must have the cleverness and forcefulness of character to override Afghan conservative, traditionalist opposition to the new approach. Finally, despite an ability to deal with the Soviets, he must be immune to their blandishments and remain a true Afghan nationalist. There was only one such individual, the forty-three-year-old Mohammed Daoud, son of the assassinated Afghan envoy to Germany and nephew of assassinated King Nader Shah.

Daoud was an authoritarian figure who believed in achieving social and economic progress by executive decree rather than democratic consensus. He had the reputation of crushing opposition with swift, ruthless efficiency, and although some trappings of democracy remained in Kabul (the parliament was not formally abolished, for example), Daoud and a few close colleagues ran the country without much recourse to debate or compromise. He appears to have concluded that simultaneous political and economic development of Afghanistan was impossible, and to have made a clear choice in favor of economic growth.[4]

Within four months of Daoud's accession to power, in the first agreement of its kind between the two countries since the early 1920s, the USSR advanced Afghanistan a $3.5 million credit for the construction of two grain silos, a flour mill, and a bakery. The terms were generous: Afghan repayment was to be made in its natural exports, wool and cotton, and was to start only three years later, on January 1, 1957; it was to consist of five equal payments bearing an interest rate of 3 percent.[5]

As an initial foray into the field of economic assistance, the Soviet project had much to recommend it: high visibility (the twenty-thousand-ton capacity grain silos in Kabul and Pul-e-Khumri are still by far the tallest structures in each town), quick results (all buildings were completed in two years), and a purpose that was both egalitarian and humanitarian (to even out the supply and hence the price of wheat over the year). On the other hand, the bakery produced a Western-style bread that was not to Afghan taste, and it absorbed a significant percentage of the meager Afghan wheat supplies.[6]

This first Soviet effort was followed in July 1954 with a technical aid and credit agreement of $1.2 million for construction of a gasoline pipeline across the Amu Darya River from the USSR and for erection of four gasoline bulk storage tanks, with a one-million-gallon total capacity, at widely dispersed points in Afghanistan.[7]

Both of these projects had clear implications for Afghanistan's ability to weather another Pashtunistan crisis like that of 1950: if Pakistan again closed the border, the silos could store strategic food reserves for the population, while the pipeline and fuel tanks could serve a similar purpose for the economy.

In August 1954, the USSR scored a propaganda coup by agreeing to finance the paving of Kabul's streets, a project that the United States Import-Export Bank had rejected a year earlier.[8] To this end the USSR advanced a $2 million credit to be used for asphalting and roadbuilding equipment. That same month the Czechs provided a $5 million, eight-year, 3 percent loan with which to build three cement plants—a project the Afghans had been trying unsuccessfully to negotiate with the Germans and Americans for two decades.[9]

While the USSR and its Czech ally were active with these projects in Afghanistan, the United States was engaged in improving Pakistan's defense potential. A U.S. military survey team arrived in Pakistan in

March 1954 to assess the country's future military needs, and before the end of the 1954 fiscal year, the United States had committed $21 million in U.S. arms aid to it.[10] In September 1954, Pakistan joined the South East Asia Treaty Organization (SEATO) and the following year it joined the Baghdad Pact (later CENTO), thus becoming a key link in the chain of mutual security pacts the United States was forging to contain Soviet expansion.

In view of their hostile relations with Pakistan, the Afghans looked with a good deal of misgiving on the U.S. support for its rival's military forces.[11] By this time, Afghanistan's closer relations with the USSR would have ruled out any Afghan participation in a regional pact aimed at containing her northern neighbor, even if there had been no tradition of nonalignment to uphold. At the same time, the United States could scarcely afford to arm an irredentist Afghanistan that had pretensions to Pakistani territory without some very good guarantees that U.S. arms were not going to be used against its security pact colleague.

Whatever the chances of U.S. arms aid to Afghanistan might have been, they were sharply reduced by a renewed eruption of violence over Pashtunistan. In the spring of 1955, Afghan mobs were permitted if not encouraged by the authorities to tear down the flag from the Pakistani Embassy in Kabul and from its consulates in Jalalabad and Kandahar and to loot those establishments. Pakistan promptly withdrew its ambassador, suspended Afghanistan's transit privileges,[12] and unleashed its own mob violence against Afghan businesses and officials in Pakistan.[13] The border remained closed for five months until the United States finally prevailed on the Pakistanis to allow transit of U.S. aid materials and equipment to the Helmand Valley.[14] The United States turned down as impractical, however, an Afghan request to build over a thousand miles of highway through Iran to give Afghanistan an alternative route to the sea.[15]

At any rate, American support for Pakistan had caused Afghan public opinion against the United States to run so high that there were threats of turning the Helmand Valley project over to Soviet engineers.[16] By contrast, the USSR enjoyed a favorable reputation: on June 28, 1955, the Afghans negotiated a new agreement on duty-free transit of Afghan goods across Soviet territory, based on Article 6 of the 1921 treaty between the two countries.[17] On August 27, 1955, the USSR implicitly guaranteed sale of Afghanistan's fruit crop (imperiled because of the Pakistani transit stoppage) by agreeing to a new barter agreement.[18]

Western analysts of the Afghan scene are divided on the interrelationship between the Pashtunistan issue and the Afghan accommodation with the USSR. Some tend to separate the two, ascribing Daoud's move toward the USSR to his desire to achieve a more truly nonaligned position by redressing a purported westward leaning of Afghan economic and political policy under Shah Mahmud. They lay the Pashtunistan propaganda to Daoud's belief that Shah Mahmud had not pushed the issue vigorously enough.[19] Others suggest that Daoud may have fostered the Pashtunistan issue deliberately for the specific purpose of justifying his turning to the USSR for economic and, especially, military aid.[20] Certainly the worsening relations with the United States must have helped overcome the trepidations of conservative Afghans regarding acceptance of assistance from the USSR.

By November Pakistan had lifted its embargo, but the way had been prepared for a quantum jump in Soviet-Afghan relations. In December 1955, at the end of a tour of southeast Asia, Nikita Khrushchev and Nikolay Bulganin, leaders of the Soviet party and the Soviet state, respectively, stopped off in Kabul. During their visit, they announced the granting of a $100 million, long-term development loan to Afghanistan. Simultaneously, the 1931 treaty of friendship and nonaggression was extended for ten years.[21]

The formal agreement was signed in January 1956. It provided for Afghan repayment to be made at the rate of 2 percent per year over twenty-two equal annual payments, with payments to start eight years after the loan was granted. Payment was to be made in Afghan goods, with prices to be determined by world market prices at the time of delivery. The nature and quantity of goods to be exchanged would be determined by mutual consent on an annual basis.[22]

It has been noted that the Soviet offer of aid to Afghanistan paralleled similar offers by the USSR to other countries during this same general time frame: 400 million rubles to Argentina in 1958, $100 million to Cuba in 1960, and one $100-million loan to Indonesia and another to Ethiopia.[23] From the perspective of the 1980s, the Soviet Union's political profit from these investments appears to have been nil in Indonesia, marginal in Argentina, and seemingly an outright success in Cuba and Ethiopia. The return on the Afghan investment is still open to question.

From the standpoint of the Afghans, acceptance of the Soviet loan violated their isolationist traditions far more significantly than had similar acceptance of American aid for the Helmand Valley project. In the 1930s Afghanistan had solicited foreign assistance on a modest scale from developed countries, but only from those whose distance from Afghanistan's borders had provided some insurance against a political/military follow-up to the economic investment. Afghan requests for German, Italian, and Japanese technological help before World War II, for example, were based less on any pro-Axis political bias than on Afghan unwillingness to give their two most powerful neighbors, the British and the Russians, any kind of economic foothold in their country. The postwar approach to the United States was based in good part on the same considerations.

As the dimensions and direction of the Soviet involvement emerged over the next months, the extent of Afghanistan's departure from established policies became ever clearer. In the 1890s Abdur Rahman had warned specifically of the dangers that a railroad would pose for his country's independence. In March 1956, the projects selected by a joint Afghan-Soviet survey team, although not involving railroads, were associated to a large extent with creating and modernizing other transportation facilities. There were two airport projects, one major highway (linking Kabul with the Soviet border), one river port facility improvement project (where the proposed highway would cross into the USSR), construction of one modern bridge, and improvement and construction of three auto repair workshops. Other projects under consideration included a materials testing laboratory in Kabul, two hydroelectric stations, three irrigation dams, and a fertilizer factory.[24] Some of these were deemed impractical and shelved.[25] That same March an air agreement was signed that provided for regular flights between Tashkent and Kabul.[26]

A curious example of Soviet defensive concerns was included in Article IV of this agreement: "Each side has the right to refuse or amend flight permission to the other if it does not have proof that the majority ownership or actual control of that enterprise is being realized by citizens or organs of that country." In other words, the burden of proof would be on Ariana Afghan Airlines to prove that it was not owned and/or controlled by a foreign concern. In fact, 49 percent of Ariana stock at that time was owned by Peter Baldwin, an American entrepreneur who actually started that airline in April 1955.[27] Later, in

1957, Pan American Airways bought out Baldwin for $400 thousand, and was active in helping Ariana with its operations and maintenance problems for more than two decades thereafter.[28]

Also in March 1956, the Afghans signed an agreement calling for Soviet specialists to be stationed in Afghanistan for the purpose of setting up, maintaining, and repairing various equipment in connection with the aid projects and training their Afghan colleagues in its use. These specialists were also supposed to oversee Afghan construction activities according to approved project plans.[29]

The greatest break with tradition, however, came with the August 1956 agreement on re-equipping Afghanistan's armed forces with Soviet matériel. Of necessity, given the complexity of modern armaments, this agreement involved the training of Afghan officers in Soviet military schools and the stationing of Soviet experts at Afghan military bases. The opportunity this gave the USSR for assessing and recruiting individual officers to serve Soviet political aims is self-evident, and it was not ignored.

Though many observers of the Afghan scene feared even then that Daoud was leading his country into Soviet vassalage, others perceived in his actions a high-risk gamble to improve his country's lot by playing off the great powers against each other. In fact, one analyst termed Afghanistan an "economic Korea," where the competition between East and West benefited a local population without endangering its independence.[30] And indeed, Afghanistan did profit in the short run as a result of competing aid programs: hardly had the agreements with the USSR been concluded in early 1956 than the United States was also offering official aid. (Before that time the Afghans had secured individual commercial loans in the West, but these were not connected with overall U.S. policy; official aid had been on a very small scale.) U.S. projects included road building, airport construction, further progress on the Helmand Valley project, and long-term educational activities (rural schools, textbooks, and the like). In addition, the United States donated one hundred thirty thousand tons of wheat to Afghanistan in the period 1956–1959, under the terms of PL-480-II, whereas in 1952–1954, before the sharp increase in Soviet aid, it had sold them just twenty thousand tons.[31]

The U.S. position in expanding the Afghan share of foreign aid was explicit. It was aimed at securing "maximum internal political stability, promoting friendly economic relations with her (Afghanistan's) Free

World neighbors, and minimizing any possibility that Afghanistan might either be a victim of, or a pathway for, Soviet domination in South Asia."[32]

In the period 1950–1959, U.S. assistance totaled $148.3 million, whereas Soviet assistance came to $246.2 million. Although most of the U.S. assistance was in the form of outright grants, the USSR concentrated more on long-term loans.[33] Although the United States did not try to match the volume of the Soviet assistance, the impact of the U.S. projects was considerable, and most Western analysts seem to feel that the Afghans benefited as much from the U.S. aid as from the Soviet.[34]

On the other hand, between 1950 and 1960 Afghan dependence on the USSR had risen from nothing to 100 percent for arms, from perhaps 10 percent to 90 percent for petroleum products, and from 17 percent (1951) to nearly 50 percent for total foreign trade.[35]

Despite the development of these strategic vulnerabilities, Afghanistan continued to maintain its nonaligned status, and Daoud made a point of emphasizing continued Afghan freedom, independence, and neutrality as leading items on his list of national priorities. Economic progress was invariably listed as a secondary aim in his speeches.[36]

During the 1950s there was little direct evidence that Soviet ambitions in Afghanistan went beyond ensuring that the country would continue to perform its traditional buffer-state role. Nevertheless, the strategic significance of the Soviet highway project that ran from the Soviet border at Kushka to Herat and Kandahar, linking up there with the U.S. highway to Kabul, was not lost on Western observers. One, who saw Soviet aims in Afghanistan as similar to those of the United States, noted that it might allow an aggressor to transport supplies and men directly to the Pakistan border—"provided he has Afghan consent."[37]

Only careful examination of agreements made during those years and of their subsequent implementation gives evidence of long-range Soviet intentions. Article 21 of the border agreement of January 18, 1958, for example, stipulated that on forty-eight-hour notice either side could examine those parts of international bridges linking the two countries that were located on the other side's territory.[38] Should the Afghans have wanted to mine these links as a defensive measure, Soviet inspectors would soon have discovered that fact. The May 30, 1959, agreement on building the Kushka-Kandahar road was followed in July by a specific agreement that dealt only with building three new bridges—across the Besuda, Kameh, and Asmar Rivers. Construction of the bridges was to involve Afghan labor working under the immediate supervision of Soviet engineers.[39] Afghan engineers were to comment subsequently on the overstrength capability of such bridges in relation to the heaviest Afghan civilian truck traffic; American military attachés commented on the odd coincidence between the bridges' load limit and the weight of the heaviest Soviet battle tank.[40]

The U.S. commitment to Afghanistan in the last years of the decade was deliberately ambiguous. In early 1957 the visit to Kabul by Special Presidential Assistant James P. Richards resulted in a communiqué that confirmed U.S. support for Afghanistan's continued independence, but did not state whether or not the country was protected by the Eisenhower Doctrine (i.e., whether it would enjoy U.S. armed support in the event of a Soviet invasion).[41]

Insofar as the USSR might have hoped for a political return on its economic investment, however, the signs were not encouraging. A visit to Kabul by President Eisenhower in December 1959 was a widely hailed success. In an obvious move to obtain equal coverage, Khrushchev visited Kabul in early 1960 and reportedly offered to finance the entire Afghan second five-year plan if the Afghans would agree to the presence of Soviet advisors in all their ministries. Daoud is said to have rejected this offer outright.[42] Not only was the United States enjoying a good reputation, but it even appeared for a short time that Afghan-Pakistani relations might be mending. A 1960 compact between the countries was designed to settle problems and bring tranquillity to the border.[43] This apparent move toward reconciliation, however, proved to be illusory.

In early 1959 the Afghan foreign minister had gone to Pakistan for talks, but the mission was not a success, and differences between the two countries again began to become more noticeable.[44] Afghan propaganda in Pakistani territory intensified, and after some delay it was countered with Pakistani propaganda beamed at Afghan listeners. As relations worsened, these exchanges evolved into official harassment (for example, Pakistani nationals were no longer issued residence permits by Afghan authorities after May 1960), and finally, in September 1960, there were armed incursions into Pakistan by Afghan irregulars disguised as tribesmen.[45] In May 1961 a similar force launched an abortive raid in support of the Nawab of Dir, on the Pakistani side of the Durand Line.[46]

In August 1961, citing Afghan harassment of its consulates in Jalalabad and Kandahar, Pakistan shut down these installations. At the same time it demanded that the Afghans close their corresponding consulates in Parichinar, Peshawar, and Quetta, on the grounds that these were fomenting sedition in Pakistan. The Afghans gave the Pakistanis a one-week ultimatum, after which, on September 6, 1961, they broke diplomatic relations. The border was again shut down, and as in the past, trade was rerouted via the USSR. Just ten days after the border closed, Daoud's brother and confidant, Sardar Mohammed Naim, flew to Moscow and returned with the promise of a Soviet airlift to export Afghanistan's perishable fruit harvest, which had been stranded by the transportation blockage.[47] Within a month, the USSR again reportedly offered Afghanistan loans and credits totaling $450 million for their second five-year plan. This was virtually the entire amount needed.[48] If this offer was indeed made, the Afghans understood its implications for the future of their independence and turned it down.

Even without their acceptance, however, the break in relations with Pakistan was clearly a desirable development from Moscow's standpoint. Afghan gratitude for the Soviet rescue of their fruit harvest was one benefit. Renewed Afghan isolation and alienation from the West was another, as U.S. aid projects faltered from the shutdown in the flow of supplies. The trend of the late 1950s toward an accommodation with Pakistan was reversed.

The extent to which the USSR might have had a hand in promoting the diplomatic break can only be conjectured. Some aspects of the conflict as it developed in the border areas along the Durand Line had a decidedly alien flavor, however.

As propaganda degenerated into actual fighting, Afghan authorities gave a bounty to Pakistani Pashtuns for each empty rifle shell and grenade pin claimed to have been used in battle against Pakistani regular forces; in addition to this, they also provided replacement munitions.[49] For Afghan authorities to have made such an offer to the hill tribesmen, who loved hunting and were customarily at war only with each other, was to display unusual naïveté, unlimited resources, or both. Furthermore, for those who wished to amass a reserve against future needs, replacement of a standard grenade pin with an old piece of wire or used cotter pin ensured a steadily mounting stock of valuable—if not entirely safe—munitions.

Those in power in Kabul were themselves Pashtuns, and could have been under no illusions as to the ultimate disposition of most of the supplies that the Afghan Army was dispensing to Pakistani Pashtuns with such a lavish hand. It is therefore not unreasonable to assume that the guarantee of the material resources to carry out this program, if not the very concept of the program itself, were of Soviet origin. In fact, the visit of Soviet Marshal Vassiliy Danilovich Sokolovskiy to Kabul in October 1961, the specific purposes of which were never made public, may have had some connection with the program.[50]

From 1961 to 1963, diplomatic relations between Afghanistan and Pakistan remained ruptured. The economic effects of the border closure were slow in coming, but eventually they began to affect the population at large. The loss of customs duty at the Pakistani border removed the single largest source of government revenues, and the country's hard currency reserves sank sharply. Eventually matters reached such a critical stage that the king asked Daoud to resign, and in March 1963, the latter obeyed.[51] Within two months diplomatic relations were re-established with Pakistan, and the border was again opened.

For the USSR, Daoud's departure was a definite setback. The goals of Soviet economic and military aid programs had been the establishment of an Afghan client-state relationship, with Kabul dependent on Moscow for marketing its exports, supplying its military forces, backing its international political claims (Pashtunistan), and modernizing its economy. On all of these issues Daoud's policies had seemed to be largely in line with Soviet aspirations, even if they had been neither avowedly nor secretly pro-Soviet.

As long as Daoud remained in power and his policies remained in force, the USSR could assume that Soviet influence would grow and Afghan dependence would increase, intensifying whenever the Pashtunistan issue became heated. In the end, it could be anticipated that the USSR would come to have a dominating political influence in the country, in both domestic and foreign relations.

For Daoud, opening the door to Soviet aid programs had been a calculated risk. It had brought increased U.S. aid to offset the Soviet effort, thus providing a double economic benefit while lessening the dangers of a total dependence on the USSR. At the same time, it had opened the door for Soviet subversion via the Afghan military forces that were trained, equipped, and advised by Soviet mentors. Daoud unquestionably recognized this danger, but apparently believed he could handle it through his own command of the army's loyalty, the patriotism of the Afghan citizenry, and the innate suspicion with which Afghans viewed Russians.

If the USSR had had any illusions that Daoud's personal ambitions outweighed his patriotism, they must have been dissipated when Daoud quietly and obediently stepped down at the request of King Zahir. This was no surprise move by the king, designed to catch Daoud off guard. On the contrary, it was deliberately floated as a rumor from the royal palace some weeks before in order to gauge the people's reaction in advance. When the response showed that a change would indeed be popular, the king made his move.

Daoud might have defied his sovereign and stayed on. He appeared to have the loyalty of the army (the ultimate source of political power in the country) and he had the time to organize a coup. If he had done so, it is difficult to imagine who could have stood in his way. Domestically he controlled the guns, and abroad he was assured of support by the USSR, the only foreign neighbor in a credible position to intervene. He chose instead to step down without resistance, but with a farewell address that did much to revive his flagging popularity among the civilian population.[52]

According to one analyst, there were three groups of people who were genuinely sorry to see Daoud step down: (1) those who ardently supported the Pashtunistan issue, (2) some members of the royal family who stood to lose lucrative positions in the government, and (3) "those few army officers and intellectuals committed to the Soviet line."[53]

From the Soviet standpoint there were few options available through which they might have salvaged their position. The logical personality around whom a coup might have been staged had removed himself from the political scene and there was no one else of any stature over whom the USSR had adequate influence. Direct military intervention was not an attractive alternative in early 1963, only a few months after the United States had faced down the USSR in Cuba, though analysts at the time did not completely rule out that possibility.[54]

Economic aid had proven to be an effective foreign policy tool, but by itself it had not been enough to establish a dominant Soviet influence in Afghanistan. For the next fifteen years the economic penetration effort would continue, but manipulation of internal *political* forces was to occupy an apparently ever more important place in Soviet strategic thinking on Afghanistan.

CHAPTER

5

The Drive for Political Control: 1

"Democratic" Political Influence

1963–1973

When Daoud took power in 1953, he established a regime that was intolerant of opposition from any quarter. The memory of the anarchic Seventh National Assembly (1949–1952) was still fresh, and Daoud's relationship even to his own ministers was less that of a senior colleague than of "a general dealing with his sergeants."[1]

As a result, an inchoate coalition of disparate elements built up against him and eventually contributed to his resignation in 1963. The very success of his program for Afghanistan's economic advancement was another contributing factor in his fall; as the economy expanded, there was an ever greater need for delegation of decisionmaking to lower and lower levels. At the same time, improvements in education had led to the formation of a larger and larger body of trained young people who wanted a voice in managing their country's affairs. One-man rule was becoming both unpopular and inefficient.

In Daoud's place, the king had appointed Mohammed Yousuf, minister of mines and industries, to take over the reins of government pending the drafting of a new constitution. In appointing Yousuf, who was no relation to himself, the king let it be known that in the future the royal family could "lay down its burden of a generation and let the Afghan educated class run the country."[2] This principle became a matter of law in Article 24 of the constitution, the fifth paragraph of which stated, "Members of the Royal House shall not hold the following offices: Prime Minister or Minister, Member of Parliament, Justice of the Supreme Court."[3]

The 1964 constitution was the final product of eighteen months of effort by a drafting commission and ten days of intense debate in a *loyah jirgah*. What emerged was a consensus document that appeared to have good prospects of success. Following its ratification and signature by the king (on October 1, 1964), the new constitution laid the groundwork for a parliamentary monarchy that included many traditional democratic principles developed in the West—separation of powers, elections by secret ballot, and presumption of innocence in court, to name a few. As in other Muslim countries, however, there was explicit linking of church and state, and for the time being civil rights received only cursory attention. Nevertheless, the constitution did provide an apparently stable base on which a democratic state could have been built. Laws governing the establishment of political parties were supposed to be developed in the first freely elected parliament, and a press law, restrictive by Western standards but very liberal in the Afghan context, was passed in July 1965. There was even provision for feminine rights in the constitution, and the *loyah jirgah* itself had four women participants.[4]

Even if there had been no group hostile to the concept of constitutional monarchy and dedicated to its overthrow, democracy would have led a perilous existence during its formative years in Afghanistan. There was at least 90 percent illiteracy in the country; communications systems were rudimentary; organizations that cut across family or tribal lines were virtually nonexistent; loyalties and hostilities alike were fierce, local, and personal; and there was no popular sense of national unity or nationwide awareness of common problems. In fact, it is surprising that the democratic experiment did manage to struggle on for ten years before again succumbing to one-man rule.

As educated Afghans wrestled with the new concepts of government, four general ideological positions emerged among the informed electorate: *traditionalists* wished to retain Afghan culture under firm, traditional Islamic principles; *adaptors* wanted somehow to meld Western technology and managerial practices with Afghan culture and Islamic teachings; *democrats* looked forward to a democratic republic and put their faith in following Western models more directly; and *Marxist-Leninists* were by definition committed in theory to eventual revolutionary overthrow of any noncommunist government.[5] With the exception of the last, all had political roots that went directly back to the World War I era of pan-Islamism and even beyond.

The first calls for representative government had come from a group called Mashruta-Khwahan (Constitutionalists) near the turn of the century. In 1909 Amir Habibullah put a temporary end to such impudence by executing many of its leaders and imprisoning the rest. Later, the Jawanan Afghan group espoused many of the same goals as the constitutionalists, and also suffered from Habibullah's wrath. Under the more liberal Amanullah, the survivors and heirs of this group re-formed and enjoyed a brief era of respectability before again being forced underground when Nader Shah seized power.[6]

After Nader Shah's assassination in 1933, there was a general hiatus in reformist political activity in Afghanistan until 1947, when renewed stirrings of interest in democratic government were felt. This time the vehicle was a group of Pashtun intellectuals headed by Ghulam Rasoud Pashtun, who eventually formalized their association as the Wikh-i-Zalmayan (Awakened Youth), another spiritual heir of Jawanan Afghan but now with a Pashtun language name and a Pashtun nationalist orientation.

In 1951 there was a veritable rash of proto-democratic political groupings and publications. Wikh-i-Zalmayan's organ *Angar* (Embers), edited by Faiz Mohammed Angar, was matched by the Watan (Homeland) group's paper *Watan*, edited by Mir Mohammed Gobar. Both competed with *Nidya-i-Khalq* (Voice of the Masses) under the editorship of Dr. Abdur Rahman Mahmudi, who was leader of the somewhat more radical—but still noncommunist—Khalq (Masses) movement. Yet a fourth political group, the Cloop-i-Melli (National Club) formed in 1950 by Prince Mohammed Daoud, had its own youth group, Etehadya Pakhtunistan (Pashtunistan Alliance), which seemed to concentrate more on keeping track of the activities of the others than pushing its own program. It counted among its members the future communist leader Babrak Karmal. All in all, these rival groups provided a surfeit of intellectual and political riches for a country with single-digit literacy.

One astonishing feature of the various movements is that in none of them can one find evidence of dominating or even serious Marxist influence. True, individuals like Nur Mohammed Taraki, eventual founder of the People's Democratic Party of Afghanistan (PDPA) and at that time a member of Wikh-i-Zalmayan, and Babrak Karmal were active in this or that group, but they acted as individuals and their ideological convictions were anything but dominating. In this respect (as in so many others) Afghanistan represents an anachronism. Whereas by 1923 all other states bordering on the USSR had full-blown Marxist-Leninist parties, legitimate or underground, more than forty years would pass before Afghanistan would enjoy that dubious gift of progress.[7]

Meantime, however, the dynamic activity of the various political groups had upset the basically conservative royal family, and the pendulum of official policy swung away from permissiveness toward repression. In 1952 Mahmudi and sixteen of his followers were arrested. Mahmudi's health was broken as a result of severe beatings by the police and prison authorities. In 1963, following Daoud's removal from power, Mahmudi was released from jail, but he died only a few months later.[8]

The year Mahmudi died was also the year Nur Mohammed Taraki began holding meetings with other leftist figures to form a new political party. Starting in September 1963, these meetings were to continue through December of the following year. They culminated in a gathering at Taraki's home in the Shah Mina district of Kabul on January 1, 1965, at which the People's Democratic Party of Afghanistan was officially founded. About thirty persons attended, twenty of whom were elected as either full or alternate members of the PDPA's Central Committee. The host, Taraki, was unanimously elected secretary general. If the gestation of organized communist political activity can be dated from Taraki's preliminary meetings, the formal birth of the Afghan communist party (even though the term communist is not used in its title) can be established as New Year's Day, 1965.

The details of what went on at the preliminary meetings are obscure; the fact that they took place at all only came to light in 1979— and in the West at that.[9] As late as 1960, an American researcher was to base his conclusion that "Soviet political aims in Afghanistan do not seem to differ much from those of the United States" in part on the fact that there is "no open or clandestine communist propaganda in Afghanistan."[10]

The specific ideological orientation of the PDPA, however, was clear from the very beginning. "Its programme," a leftist journal was to report later, "was an orthodox Communist one for the period, reflecting analyses associated with Khrushchev or Brezhnev."[11] Later, its official organ, *Khalq*, was to declare the PDPA's goal as the "further development of the great October Revolution in Afghanistan."[12] Given the PDPA's unswerving subsequent support to any and all Soviet initiatives, the source of its inspiration would not have been difficult to deduce even without this declaration.

Following its formation as an organization, the PDPA was quick to apply its revolutionary doctrine. By the end of the following summer, elections to the lower house of parliament (Wolesi Jirgah) had resulted in victories for a few PDPA officials, including Central Committee members Babrak Karmal, Anahita Ratebzad (one of four women elected to the lower house), and Nur Ahmad Nur. Nur Mohammed Taraki and Hafizullah Amin ran but did not win their contests. Due to the numerical insignificance of leftist representation in parliament, PDPA policy was to sabotage that body's work rather than to operate within it.

Pending convocation of parliament, the king had continued to put his faith in Mohammed Yousuf, the interim prime minister who had been acting since Daoud's departure in 1963. After the elections, the king asked Yousuf to form a new government, which he did. When the new government was presented to parliament for confirmation, however, the proposed ministers were subjected to several days of unbridled abuse by the newly elected members. Babrak and Anahita led the anti-Yousuf protest, which reached such a pitch of vituperation that Yousuf finally asked that either formal charges be leveled against him and his ministers in a court of law, or an end be called to the denunciations that had included charges of bribery, corruption, nepotism, and the like. He requested that his new cabinet be subjected to a vote of confidence in three days' time.[13]

If the vote had been taken immediately, Dr. Yousuf might well have won it without difficulty. As it was, three days was adequate for Babrak to mobilize his sympathizers among the Kabul student body. A student sit-in staged by him and his supporters forced parliament to cancel a scheduled meeting on October 24, the day the new cabinet was to be approved. The following day, parliament met in closed session, and overwhelmingly voted in favor of the Yousuf government. The fact that the session was closed, however, touched off riots in which three students were killed. Yousuf immediately resigned, and on October 29 parliament elected Mohammed Hashim Maiwandwal as prime minister in his place. (Only seven votes were cast against the choice of Maiwandwal; true to the PDPA policy of disruption, the same seven votes were to be the only ones registered against Prime Minister Etemadi in a vote of confidence in 1967.[14])

The student riots were a development that set back the cause of democracy in Afghanistan perhaps more than any other single event in the 1960s. The extent to which the USSR had a direct hand in the riots is open to question. Certainly the PDPA took its overall ideological guidance from Moscow, and it is reasonable to assume that there was local PDPA contact with the Soviet embassy in Kabul to decide immediate questions of tactics and strategy. This does not necessarily imply a fully coordinated Soviet control over the PDPA, however, and there is some evidence that the USSR was embarrassed vis-à-vis the Third World by the violent turn the demonstrations took. In 1966 one Soviet author, writing in English (i.e., for non-Soviet audiences), euphemistically referred to the riots only as "actions of an oppositionist nature . . . [that] caused certain difficulties in forming the new cabinet."[15] On the other hand, the same author, writing this time in Russian for Soviet audiences, dealt with the riots less elliptically and with some implicit approval, noting that they followed Leninist teachings on the revolutionary role of the intelligentsia.[16]

Although the new prime minister managed to become popular among the students by appearing at the memorial service for those who had been killed, PDPA agitation in the student body resulted in new violence before the end of the year. Starting on December 9, leftist leaders instigated anti-German demonstrations, aimed against the West German educational assistance program and alleged misconduct by West German visiting educators in the science faculty at Kabul University.[17] These demonstrations met with generally tepid support by the student body at large, even though the December 12 sentencing to two years in prison for a leftist teacher, Mohammed Osman, also from the science faculty, provided a new focus for unrest.

The Germans have generally been popular among Afghans, and the anti-German demands made by the student agitators were considered unrealistic by most students and by the population at large.[18] The role of the West Germans as whipping boys for Soviet propagandists of that day, however, may explain this ill-advised choice of target by the agitators.

Following an initial period of uncertainty, the Afghan government's response to the unrest was a forthright program of arrests and expulsions from the university of persons thought to have been responsible for fomenting disturbances. This policy had the desired sobering effect on the students in the short term, but it was at the expense of slowing and even reversing the process of democratization in the country.

In the spring of 1966, reaction against the government took a new form as six opposition newspapers came into being in response to relaxation of government censorship regulations. Only one of the six was clearly identifiable as a communist journal. This was *Khalq* (Masses), published by the PDPA's secretary general, Nur Mohammed Taraki, and edited by Bareq Shafiee, a durable figure in PDPA politics.

If there had been any previous doubts as to the politico-ideological orientation of the PDPA, they should have been laid to rest by *Khalq*. Even the phraseology of its writings was alien to Afghan Persian, resembling that found in political organs in Soviet Tadzhikistan.[19] As for content, the paper followed the Soviet line both in general ideological terms ("the main issue of contemporary times and the center of class struggle on a world-wide basis is the struggle between international socialism and international imperialism, which began with the Great October Revolution") and even on such specific Soviet dogmas as the demand for socialist realism in art.[20]

The government moved quickly to suppress what it identified as a subversive journal; after six issues *Khalq* was shut down. The reasons cited were the paper's anti-Islam, antimonarchy, and anticonstitution lines, but it is probable that the government's real concern was its identification of *Khalq* as little less than a controlled Soviet outlet operating on Afghan territory. As in the case of leftist-sponsored riots the previous October, the strong countermeasures taken by the government injured more than just the truly alien target. Of the six opposition journals that appeared in the first half of 1966, only one remained at the end of the year. One had closed for financial reasons, one (founded to fight *Khalq*) ceased publication because its reason for existence had been removed, and three were shut down by government decree.[21]

After *Khalq*'s demise there was no officially sanctioned communist journal until Sulaiman Laeq began publishing *Parcham* (Banner) in March 1968. Laeq's coeditor on *Parcham* was Mir Akbar Khyber (whose assassination ten years later was to trigger the 1978 communist coup), but its unacknowledged chief was Babrak Karmal.

In June 1967, the PDPA formally split into two hostile factions: the Khalqis under Nur Mohammed Taraki and the Parchamis under Babrak. There was no real ideological reason for the break: both Taraki and Babrak remained firmly loyal to Soviet-style Marxism-Leninism, and differed mainly as to tactics.[22]

The Khalqis put emphasis on class warfare, while the Parchamis called for a united democratic front that was supposed to work within the framework of the existing order. Both of these lines, of course, reflect tactics that Communist parties in most countries have pursued at various times without ever losing sight of the ultimate strategic goal of permanently displacing the indigenous noncommunist government. In the case of Parcham and Khalq, even these differences were minor: in 1966 *Khalq* (Taraki's paper) recognized the need for the monarchy "at this stage of Afghanistan's development," scarcely a class war position.[23] For his part, Babrak gave away nothing in his efforts to gain noncommunist political allies in a united front. It must also be recalled that Babrak had been the "class warrior" who had called the students out to disrupt Parliament, whereas Taraki, whatever his professed revolutionary convictions, was essentially a poet and an intellectual, not an activist.

Similarly, a purported difference in commitment to Pashtunistan (backed more consistently by the Khalqis) was more apparent than real. Inasmuch as the Khalqis were predominantly Pashtun, while the Parchamis were more representative of all Afghan nationalities, such a difference would have been natural in any case. In fact, however, when Parchamis found it politically expedient to support Pashtunistan, they did so with as much vigor as the Khalqis.

Babrak and Taraki each commanded the loyalty of about half of the PDPA movement, and each was to maintain an unbroken hostility toward the other for ten years—until 1977, when a seeming reconciliation, imposed from the outside by the USSR, took place. During all this time each maintained firm loyalty to Moscow while accusing the other of various deviations. The fundamental reason for their hostility was the personal antagonism and rivalry for control of the party between the two leaders. Only after this had developed were somewhat artificial ideological and tactical differences brought out as ostensible explanations for the split.

In 1968 a new wave of labor strikes and student unrest swept over the country. Again, the degree to which the USSR was directly involved cannot be determined, but neither Khalq not Parcham was an idle bystander to the violence that erupted. In part as a reaction to these disturbances, a purported massive shift to the right occurred in the 1969 parliamentary elections.[24] For the period of the election, *Parcham* and several other opposition newspapers were banned, and there were subsequent allegations that the government interfered blatantly to secure the defeat of leftist candidates.[25] Insofar as the government may have indulged in such activities, it does not seem to have pressed its campaign with great vigor. Although Nur Ahmad Nur, who dates his PDPA membership from 1963,[26] was defeated, and Anahita Ratebzad did not run, Hafizullah Amin (defeated in 1965) did win and Babrak himself was re-elected. Overall, the left did lose ground, but the cause was probably less a matter of government interference than the weakening effect of the Parcham/Khalq split, on the one hand, and popular reaction against leftist disturbances, on the other.

The left's popularity was further eroded when, in April 1970, *Parcham* printed an ode to Lenin on the occasion of his birthday, praising him in terms normally reserved for the Prophet Mohammed. This resulted in anticommunist demonstrations by mullahs and their followers, which were met by student counterdemonstrations. The poet responsible for the ode was Bareq Shafiee, who had been editor of *Khalq* under Taraki in 1966, was working for Babrak on *Parcham* at the time of this poem, was to be minister of transport and tourism under Taraki in 1979, and as of June 1980, was again a ranking figure in the PDPA under Babrak. Such changes in allegiance are unusual and are considered improper by most Afghans; a possible reflection of this attitude is the fact that Shafiee, despite his earlier prominence in the movement, was accorded only *alternate* membership in the 1980 Babrak Central Committee and Revolutionary Council.

As the decade of the 1960s came to an end, Afghanistan's importance as an overt area for playing out the East-West struggle seems to have waned, as Vietnam came ever more to dominate the international scene. Year by year the Soviet economic investment in Afghanistan was cut back, from $44.7 million in 1967–68, to $30.5 million in 1968–69, to $28.4 million in 1969–70. During the same period, U.S. grants and loans fell even faster, from $12.7 million, to $4.8 million, to $1.4 million.[27]

Politically, those forces in Afghanistan that publicly supported the

USSR became less popular. Despite its publication of the near-heretical ode to Lenin, *Parcham* was allowed to continue publication, but it did not command a large readership. Leftist strength in the Wolesi Jirgah was negligible. The prospects for a communist victory in any free election were virtually nonexistent in the foreseeable future.

These trends led some analysts to conclude that the importance of Afghanistan had been reduced in Soviet eyes. While this apparent loss of interest was developing, however, Afghan civilian students and military officers continued to be trained in the Soviet Union, where they were bombarded with Soviet propaganda and fell under long-term scrutiny of the Soviet intelligence services. At the same time, the decrease in foreign aid had led to unemployment among the restless new intelligentsia that was being turned out in ever larger numbers by the expanded educational program. Afghanistan's fragile democracy appeared progressively less capable of handling the complex problems of a rapidly developing economy.

It is doubtful that long-term Soviet political plans in Afghanistan had changed between 1963 and 1973. Reliance on "democratic" political instruments (the PDPA, *Khalq*, and *Parcham*), however, had proven as ineffectual an approach for the USSR as reliance on purely economic penetration had shown itself during the previous decade. It was time for a new approach, one that might result in effective Soviet influence on the country's policies from behind the scenes.

The end of democracy in Afghanistan came on July 17, 1973, when Mohammed Daoud again took over the country, this time in a nearly bloodless coup that saw the king banished into exile, the constitution abrogated, and civil liberties suspended. Afghanistan had returned to one-man rule.

CHAPTER

6

The Drive for Political Control: 2

Political Manipulation

1973–1978

When Mohammed Daoud came to power for the second time, his takeover was virtually unopposed. The only casualties were one tank commander (who drowned when his vehicle swerved off the road to avoid collision with a bus and sank in the Kabul River), and seven policemen at one station (all of whom mistook the rebels for some other hostile force). Within hours the country was securely in Daoud's hands, and there was no armed opposition to the coup. The king was in Europe at the time, and he simply stayed there, accepting exile in Italy.

Daoud's swift success can be ascribed to classic coup prerequisites: disaffection with the existing regime by key elements of the population, his own correct perception of the government's vulnerability to overthrow, secure advance planning by the conspirators, and assurances by the military that the nation's armed forces would either remain neutral or support the coup.

The popular dissatisfactions with the monarchy were vague but pervasive. Not only were such corrupt practices as bribe-taking and nepotism flourishing as much under the *Democracy-i-nau* (New Democracy) as they had under earlier regimes, but the very freedom to expose and criticize such practices (without being able to stop them) led to even greater popular discontent than before.

Daoud also recognized the factors that made democracy so frail in Afghanistan—lack of communications, low literacy rate, and the like.

Perhaps the single most important weakness was the absence of any pan-Afghan organizations that would have permitted appreciation of truly national problems and inculcated in the people loyalties beyond the immediate calls of family and tribe. Political parties eventually might have filled this gap, but the only such organizations in existence in 1973 were still embryonic—the quasi-legal PDPA factions (Parcham and Khalq), the Maoist Sholaye Jaweid (Eternal Flame), and Mohammed Hashim Maiwandwal's unofficial Progressive Democratic Party (PDP), for example. Government failure to get on with passing a political parties law is in part to blame for this situation, but it is doubtful that even legal sanction would have permitted a rapid enough development of various party organizations and loyalties to have forestalled the 1973 coup.[1]

The third and probably decisive factor was the coterie of supporters that had gravitated to Daoud during the years since his last term of office. Starting in 1969, he began holding seminars to discuss what had gone wrong during his previous tenure and what might be done to correct both his own former errors and those of the present regime. Young military officers, many of them trained in the USSR and already members of Parcham or Khalq, attended these meetings, as did more moderate thinkers.[2] From the cabinet Daoud put together when the coup succeeded, it appears that most of the members of his previous (1953–1963) government were ignored in the planning for his new one. Excluding his younger brother Naim (who throughout Daoud's career remained a close foreign policy advisor, with or without a formal title), the only carry-over of ministerial rank from the 1953–1963 era was Dr. Abdul Majid (minister of education in 1952–1957 and minister of justice 1973–1977).

In place of his former ministers Daoud appointed new people, most of them unknown on the Afghan political scene, though some had already had unpublicized experience in government. (Mohammed Hassan Sharq, for example, first deputy prime minister under Daoud in 1973, had been head of the Prime Ministry Secretariat from 1953 to 1963,[3] yet his biography is not to be found in Adamec's authoritative Who's Who of Afghanistan.)

Although none of these men had been a PDPA Central Committee member or alternate in 1965, no fewer than eight out of fourteen were known—then or later—as PDPA members, former members, or strong sympathizers. This category included the only two officials of ministerial rank to carry over from the previous (Shafiq) government to Daoud's without demotion. Six of the eight leftists were to hold important positions in government under Babrak Karmal in 1980: two were to be ministers; three, ambassadors; and one, advisor to the Prime Ministry. Of the other two, one was killed in the 1978 coup and the other has dropped from sight.

Not ideology but military power brought Daoud to power. He had the loyalty of key military officers, and he exploited that fact in carrying out the coup. Here again, the individuals who helped him were for the most part pro-Soviet. Of those who featured in the coup, only General Abdul Mustaghni, Major Abdul Qadir Nuristani, and Colonel Ghulam Sarwar had no leftist affiliations. Three of the pro-Soviet military officers (Pacha Gul Wafadar, Faiz Mohammed, and Abdul Hamid Mohtat) quit the army after the coup and joined Daoud's first cabinet as ministers, while four others (Abdul Qader, Mohammed Aslam Watanjar, Sayed Mohammed Gulabzoy, and Sher Jan Mazdooryar) remained on as career soldiers. The latter were to play key roles in the 1978 coup that toppled Daoud himself. All seven of them, civilian and military alike, were ranking members of the communist regime in 1980. In 1973, however, they had been the key to Daoud's success.

In addition to the formal organs of state administration, Daoud's government contained a somewhat mysterious Central Committee whose functions and complete membership were never spelled out, but which seemed to act in a policy advisory role for Daoud. Of six members listed in one compilation, all but Daoud himself had pasts and/or futures of close affiliation with Marxism-Leninism.[4]

Daoud had one other very important tactical advantage. Shafiq's minister of interior, Nehmatullah Pazhwak, was a secret Parcham adherent.[5] In the two years he had served as minister of interior, Pazhwak had hired a number of young Parcham activists as policemen and as other Interior Ministry officials in Kabul. There were, in Kabul, about 160 of these young enthusiasts on whom Daoud could count for support in the first days of his new government.

In addition to helping Daoud after he took over, Pazhwak had also been in a position both to affect government policy under Shafiq and to betray it. This may serve to explain why General Abdul Wali, chief of Central Forces under the king, took no action to thwart the Daoud conspirators, a list of whose identities and a description of whose intentions were reportedly in his hands at least twenty-four hours

before the coup; he allegedly was led to believe that the coup was
scheduled for some time later in the year.[6] As minister of interior, with
concomitant security responsibilities, Pazhwak was in a good position
both to warn Daoud that his conspirators' identities and plans had
been compromised and to mislead Abdul Wali as to the date of the
probable coup.

With this kind of leftist involvement, there is no doubt that the
Soviets were at least aware of Daoud's plans in advance, if indeed they
did not actively promote them for their own purposes. There would
have been every reason for them to assist him in seizing power.

In Mohammed Daoud the USSR had a prospective figurehead chief
of state whose noncommunist credentials were impeccable: as a first
cousin of the monarch he wished to depose, and as a former prime
minister who had demonstrated his true nonalignment by encouraging
both Soviet and American aid, Daoud would scarcely call forth any
strong American objection if he took over. At the same time, the
opportunities for Soviet influence in Afghan affairs would be strengthened immeasurably by the coterie of Parchamis and Khalqis surrounding him. Not only might they influence Afghan policies in directions
favorable to Soviet interests, but it could be done without any Soviet
ideological commitment or responsibility for the actions of the "noncommunist" Afghan government.

This factor was especially important for the Soviets in relation to the
Pashtunistan issue. Ever since Daoud left power in 1963, the Afghan
monarchy had made consistent efforts to downplay Pashtunistan and to
keep relations with Pakistan as cordial as possible. In 1973, with the
re-formation of the former East and West Pakistans into Bangladesh
and Pakistan, respectively, there was a clear opportunity for further
weakening the already somewhat insecure government in Islamabad.[7]

From the Soviet standpoint, to ignore such a potential would be to
miss an opportunity to undermine a friend of China and an ally of the
United States. At the same time, the Soviet Union had to play a
delicate game in this regard, for it did not wish to offend other Islamic
states with which it had good relations. In Daoud, the USSR had a
proxy for helping to destabilize Pakistan without the USSR having to
take responsibility for such activity. Daoud's own well-known dedica-
tion to Pashtunistan would be enough to mask any Soviet involvement.

A somewhat similar situation existed with respect to Iran. The
Shafiq government had reached an agreement with Iran over allocation

of the Helmand River waters so necessary for irrigating both Afghan and Iranian territory. Some Afghans, supported if not led and inspired by Parcham and Khalq, insisted that the monarchy had sold out Afghan water rights to the Iranians. At the same time, the fact that some Baluchi tribesmen (included as part of the Pashtunistan issue) inhabited southeastern Iran automatically extended that problem into Iranian territory. Again, the USSR had every motive for embarrassing a U.S. ally (Iran being at that time the strongest bulwark of anticommunist defense in the Middle East) without itself taking responsibility for hurting an Islamic power.

Finally, regardless of the results inside Iran or Pakistan, abrasive Afghan behavior could be counted on to alienate Afghanistan from the West and by default drive it into a closer relationship with the USSR.

The need for action from the Soviet standpoint was immediate. Ever since the 1969 elections, and especially since the Shafiq government's crackdown on dissidents, leftist strength (although occasionally showing itself in student demonstrations and strikes) had been waning.[8] By contrast, Western influence, despite a fall-off in U.S. government aid, appeared to be growing. The establishment of a Western-sponsored Industrial Development Bank of Afghanistan in March 1973, for example, was designed to allow a multinational bank consortium from France, Britain, the United States, and Japan to take on a 40 percent interest in development in the country. (The other 60 percent was to be in Afghan hands.)

Worse, from the Soviet view, former Prime Minister Maiwandwal was building an ever more organized political party of his own, the Progressive Democratic Party (PDP), which was not at all in line with Soviet interests. The PDP envisaged creation of a firmly Islamic constitutional monarchy in Afghanistan, one that would evolve progressively into a social democracy after building a strong nationalist pan-Afghan ethos.[9]

Worst of all, Maiwandwal, along with forty-five noncommunist military officers, had been planning his own coup d'état against the Shafiq government. The timing for this is not known, but presumably it would have occurred later in 1973 if Daoud had not struck first. When Daoud's coup came, Maiwandwal was in Iraq on the last leg of a journey that had included stops in Moscow and Western Europe. While in Moscow he apparently sounded out Soviet leaders on what their reactions would be if the PDP were to come to power legally in the elections that were scheduled for that August and September. The Soviet reply was equivocal.[10] Given the state of Soviet espionage in Afghanistan, it is not unlikely that the Kremlin was aware of his coup plans as well. If so, there was good reason for the Soviets to prompt their adherents in Daoud's entourage to move ahead with dispatch to pre-empt the coup option.

In Maiwandwal the Soviets must have recognized a threat to their long-term plans in Afghanistan. Even after Daoud succeeded, that threat remained. Not only was Maiwandwal a politically popular figure in Afghanistan as well as abroad, but his relations with Daoud and Naim were excellent. He had been Naim's protégé in the Foreign Ministry, and there was speculation that Daoud would groom him as a successor to his own leadership role. He would have been a powerful figure in any democratic government, and he thus represented a threat to the left.[11]

On return to Kabul from his trip, Maiwandwal held several long conversations with the two brothers, and his political future seemed bright. Within days, however, he was under arrest for allegedly plotting against the new regime, along with his previous co-conspirators against the Shafiq government. Although there were reports that he had tried to dissuade his colleagues from taking any action against Daoud's government on the grounds that it deserved a chance to prove itself, tape recordings of purported conversations between him and the other conspirators were played for Daoud and convinced him of Maiwandwal's guilt. Maiwandwal was held incommunicado for several months, and then strangled in his cell by two "extreme leftists" on the night of October 20, 1973. Supposedly neither Daoud nor Naim had desired any harm to come to Maiwandwal, but they authorized the official cover-up story that he had committed suicide. Furthermore, Maiwandwal was later sentenced to death posthumously by the court that tried his colleagues.[12]

With Maiwandwal safely neutralized within days after the coup, the USSR could be forgiven for looking with some complacency on the Afghan situation. There was a predominance of leftists in the Daoud cabinet; a leftist-dominated Central Committee was giving advice behind the scenes; a group of leftist military officers was taking over the key military positions; and the Ministry of Interior (especially its police element) had been significantly penetrated by young Parchami officers.

The Soviets, however, had reckoned without the political acumen of the supposed figurehead, Sardar Mohammed Daoud.

Daoud's first move was to dissipate the dangerous concentration of Parchamis in the Ministry of Interior. Although the minister himself, Pazhwak, had been a valuable asset in the coup, he was transferred immediately to the politically less important position of minister of education. Daoud then broke up the Parchami nucleus by sending all 160 of them out into the Afghan rural districts with instructions to promote their progressive theories at the grass-roots level.[13]

Although some Afghans were worried at the time that this move proved Daoud's leftist orientation and represented a genuine effort by him to spread Marxism, the reverse was almost certainly the case. Daoud understood his countrymen and the impossibility of altering traditional patterns of country life without applying draconian methods. These methods he withheld from the young Parchamis, whose efforts to breach the "mud curtain" of rural Afghanistan were thus doomed to failure. Out of communication with each other and with the capital, they ceased to exist as a potential political force. Those who quit their posts and tried to return to Kabul were dealt with severely, losing their jobs (and sometimes even their freedom) for dereliction of duty.

Daoud's next move was more cautious and deliberate, but it was certainly unwelcome from the leftist viewpoint. Several months after taking power, he began reappointing his leftist ministers to new, less important positions. Daoud himself personally held the vital portfolios of defense and foreign affairs, but leftists controlled a significant portion of the rest of his cabinet.

First to go was Pacha Gul Wafadar, an air force engineer who had been trained in the USSR, and who in March 1974 was relieved of his duties as minister of frontier and tribal affairs (a somewhat sensitive post in view of the Pashtunistan issue). He was posted with honor as ambassador to Bulgaria, but the "true" story of the transfer was leaked by the government and soon became common knowledge. He had secretly married a Soviet girl while in training in the USSR, and after the coup, he had brought her back to Afghanistan on the assumption that the old regulations prohibiting such liaisons had died with the monarchy. Daoud's punishment was to transfer him out of the country. The fact that he was a leftist ostensibly had no bearing on the matter.

Next, in April 1974, Abdul Hamid Mohtat, minister of communications, was dismissed abruptly. Like Pacha Gul Wafadar, he had been a member of the Central Committee as well as a minister. Unlike the latter, when he was fired from the ministry he lost his Central Committee membership as well, and received no other appointment. The reason given for his expulsion was his failure to "follow the policy of the State and the fundamentals of the Central Committee," a charge no more enlightening today than it was in 1974.[14] The fact that Mohtat was posted as ambassador to Japan by both Khalq and Parcham communist governments does, however, offer implicit evidence that his allegiances have been consistently Marxist-Leninist.

In December 1974, Pazhwak was dismissed as minister of education, and nine months later, in September 1975, Daoud downgraded Faiz Mohammed from the key post of minister of interior to minister of frontier and tribal affairs, while at the same time he dismissed Ghulam Jailani Bakhtari as minister of agriculture. As if fearing that such humiliation of two leftists at once might arouse Soviet ire, Daoud simultaneously raised Minister of Finance Sayyid Abdulellah's status to that of second deputy prime minister.[15]

By early 1977, Abdulellah was the only man left in Daoud's cabinet with any known history of Parcham connections, although Minister of Commerce Mohammed Khan Jalalar (who was to receive the same portfolio under Babrak in 1980) was even then suspected by many Afghans of being secretly in league with the Soviets.[16] Faiz Mohammed had been posted as ambassador to Indonesia in September 1976, and in 1977 Hassan Sharq—the last of the well-known leftists—went to Japan in the same capacity.

If Daoud had moved swiftly against the young Parchamis in the Ministry of Interior and cautiously against his own leftist ministers, he was doubly cautious when it came to the military. This was where the real political power of the country lay and Daoud could not afford to offend any group within it. At the same time, it had been Daoud who, in his earlier term of office, had given the military the prestige that it enjoyed in 1973, and he appears to have believed that the key officers owed true allegiance to him. This belief was to prove a fatal error on his part in 1978.

Before that time, however, he appears to have entertained doubts about the loyalty of specific individuals in sensitive positions. For example, Captain Zia Mohammedzai Zia, commander of the Republican Guard, an elite detachment responsible for protecting the prime minister and other ranking government figures, was a well-known Parchami. Despite his modest rank, Zia commanded about two thousand highly trained troops who held the power of life and death over those whom they were supposed to protect. In 1975, Daoud promoted Zia to major, and then at the end of that year to lieutenant colonel—but simultaneously he posted him to New Delhi as military attaché. Zia was replaced by a lower-ranking but thoroughly loyal officer, Sahib Jan.

Another officer removed from a strategic post was Lieutenant Colonel Abdul Qader, who had led the air force in support of Daoud in 1973. At first appointed chief of staff for the air force, he was demoted and transferred for public criticism of Daoud. (He was restored to his former post in 1977.)[17]

The other officers were mostly left in place, including Captain (later Major) Mohammed Aslam Watanjar (who had commanded a key armored force in support of Daoud), Captain Sayed Mohammed Gulabzoy, and Major Sher Jan Mazdooryar. Like Qader, each of these three had received training in the USSR, each was to command troops against Daoud in 1978, and each was to receive a ministerial post in Taraki's communist government as a reward.[18] As long as such key leftist military figures remained in place, the USSR could feel (with good reason) that its ultimate interests in the country were being protected. With Daoud's one-man rule in effect, his departure from the scene for any reason—a coup led by the right or left, or merely the toll of his years—would leave the field open for a takeover by pro-Soviet elements in the army. The Maoist dictum that political power grows from gun barrels was and is a stark reality in a country with political institutions as underdeveloped as those in Afghanistan. This is a fact likely to be appreciated by those who, like the Soviets, saw their own immediate political forebears rise to power by force of arms.

Meanwhile, in the international arena, Daoud was taking a series of steps that were not in line with Soviet objectives. Initially, in 1973–1974, he reverted to traditionally aggressive Afghan policies on Pashtunistan. This, as has been noted, was fully in line with Soviet policies designed to disrupt and destabilize Pakistan, especially now that the latter was emerging as one of China's new allies.

By early 1975, however, Kabul was making quiet overtures to Islamabad to defuse the problem. These efforts continued for over a year before they culminated, in the summer of 1976, in exchange visits between presidents Ali Bhutto and Mohammed Daoud. A Pakistani gesture that helped mollify Afghan public opinion was the offer of generous aid to alleviate suffering caused by a severe earthquake and floods in northern Afghanistan in early 1976. By August 31, 1976 (Pashtunistan Day in Afghanistan), relations had improved to such a degree that this traditional occasion for inflammatory anti-Pakistan agitation and propaganda passed in Kabul almost without public notice.[19]

Of equal concern to Moscow must have been Afghanistan's rapprochement with Iran. In July 1974, a year after the coup, Afghanistan signed a new development agreement under which Iran would finance transportation and industrial projects, including a railroad, whose total value was then estimated at $1 billion.[20] Later, the shah was to promise Afghanistan $2 billion for its seven-year plan. This was more than the total aid proffered by all foreign donors since World War II,[21] though falling oil revenues may have caused the Iranians subsequently to back off on this commitment to some degree.[22] Whatever hopes the USSR might have had for reaping political benefits from its own continuing economic aid would have been dissipated if the Iranian projects had all gone forward. Few of them did, however, and most of the promised aid remained unrealized. It was inordinately difficult for Iranians and Afghans to reach agreement on projects during this period. One wonders whether the USSR was actively involved in trying to sabotage them. With Jalalar as minister of commerce and Abdulellah as minister of finance, there may have been opportunities for complicating negotiations; if so, it is hard to believe that they would have been overlooked.

Even without Iranian investments, Afghanistan was diversifying its requests for aid in other directions. Saudi Arabia, India, and China were among those countries that responded, and the influence of Soviet aid projects dropped proportionately.

Taken in sum, all of the foregoing developments ran counter to Moscow's interests. Even the Afghan political vulnerability to future coups, ensured by the one-man nature of Daoud's rule, appeared to be diminishing. In January 1977, after a year of quiet preparatory work, a constitutional commission presented its findings to a *loyah jirgah*. This was the first representative assembly convened since Daoud's assumption of power for the second time. Three weeks of substantive and vigorous debate on the commission's draft document produced a constitution that appeared to fit Afghanistan's needs.[23] An optimist could have looked forward to the development of a stable nation-state with a growing immunity to violent overthrow.

Although Soviet official propaganda still avoided criticism of the Daoud regime, Soviet displeasure with Afghanistan's policies was displayed in early 1977 during a trip by Daoud and Naim to Moscow. In a brief, hostile exchange, Brezhnev suddenly challenged Daoud to "get rid of all those imperialist advisors in your country." Daoud replied coldly that when Afghanistan had no further need of foreign advisors, they would *all* be asked to leave. Naim ascribed more significance to this exchange than did Daoud, who took it as nothing more than a typical Soviet gambit, designed to put him on the defensive.[24]

In early summer of 1977, the Khalq and Parcham factions of the old PDPA were officially reconciled and a new PDPA organization was formed.[25] The significance of this reunification, temporary as it turned out to be, is hard to overestimate, yet it went largely unnoticed (or was reported in distorted form) by Western students of Afghanistan until after the 1978 coup. Although there is and can be no absolute proof of Soviet involvement in the rapprochement, the intensity of the Khalq-Parcham rivalry was always such that it is hard to conceive of the two parties having reached an agreement without outside pressure. Though such temporary accommodation between rival factions is not unusual in the West, the Afghan tradition of sworn enmity is one of the strongest in the whole culture. Only the application of some overriding force is likely to submerge such personal animosities as those that existed between Babrak and Taraki. The implication is that the USSR stepped in to heal the breach, and that serious, detailed coup plotting—with or without immediate Soviet guidance—can be dated from that event.

Through the balance of 1977, Daoud appeared to be relying ever more heavily on a small inner cabinet of advisors who seemed to have replaced the former, pro-Soviet Central Committee. The only member of this group who had any record of association with Parcham was Abdulellah. Only in April 1978, days before his death, did Daoud seem to be ready to open up the advisory group to a wider spectrum of political thought and technical expertise, even reviving the name Central Committee. By then it was too late.[26]

In the meantime, a series of apparently political assassinations had occurred in Kabul. In August 1977 a pilot of the Afghan national airlines (Ariana), who had been instrumental in leading a successful strike, was shot to death outside his apartment. The pilot resembled Babrak and was his neighbor, leading to speculation that he might have been a victim of mistaken identity. In November, the apparently apolitical minister of planning, Ahmad Ali Khoram, was marched at gunpoint by a solitary assassin from his office to a public square where he was killed. The killer confessed under torture to having fifty-four colleagues who were allegedly involved in a plot to assassinate Daoud and his cabinet. The government said that he had been trained outside Afghanistan, but provided no further details.[27] These killings have not been solved, and it is questionable whether either one really was political.

The final assassination, however, became political whether or not it was originally intended to be so. On the night of April 17, 1978, Mir Akbar Khyber, a well-known Parcham ideologue and one of the founding editors of *Parcham*, was murdered by one or more persons later identified as khalqis. Two days later, the PDPA, blaming that assassination on the CIA, staged a surprisingly large demonstration of some ten to fifteen thousand marchers for Khyber's funeral.[28] Daoud moved swiftly to arrest leading leftists, but his actions were not decisive enough: there was no concerted move against leftist military officers and Hafizullah Amin, the pivotal Khalqi organizer of military cadres, was held only under house arrest for a critical ten-and-a-half-hour period at the start of the police sweep.

These tactical errors were to cost Daoud his life within the next twenty-four hours, and ultimately they cost Afghanistan its national independence. One must question how much longer the Soviets would have allowed Daoud and his regime to survive anyway. By 1977 the USSR must have realized that he could not be manipulated, and from then on it was just a matter of time before they took steps to establish a government more amenable to Soviet aims and control.

In giving up its effort at covert manipulation, however, the USSR had to pay a price. Although the PDPA stoutly affirmed its nationalist and independent nonalignment, that line was difficult to put across convincingly. The PDPA's Marxist-Leninist orientation was too well known, and Soviet intentions toward the country were emerging ever more obviously, in spite of continuing efforts to mask them.

CHAPTER

7

The Drive for
Political Control: 3

Rule by Communist Party Proxy
May 1978–August 1979

To the foreign observer who is not directly aiding a coup conspiracy, the coup itself almost always comes as a surprise. It can scarcely be otherwise, for if a disinterested outsider is aware of the plotting, so in all likelihood are the security organs of the regime that hopes to stay in power. Coups, therefore, must be designed in secret, with knowledge of the full plan restricted to the smallest possible group of leaders, individual details portioned out carefully only to those with the most essential need to know, and the one vital detail, the timing, held secret until the last possible moment.

Thus it usually requires time for most foreign governments to react to the fact of a coup and to assess the survival potential of the new government before rushing to extend recognition. In 1978, as in 1973, the first country to recognize the new Afghan government was the USSR. The suspicion that the Soviets had foreknowledge of the 1978 coup is heightened by the fact that Soviet recognition came on Sunday, April 30, in the middle of the long weekend celebrations for May Day. Interestingly, the announcement came first from Kabul, and was still unconfirmed in Moscow on May 1.[1]

The 1978 coup had several unusual aspects. The first was the PDPA claim that it drilled its military members beforehand in their duties with great thoroughness, holding some ten rehearsals! It was able to run such drills without compromise because it camouflaged them (by means that have not been spelled out openly) so that "had Daoud been intimated [sic] he would not have suspected any of the measures against his regime."[2] Whatever the cover, it was clearly adequate and the drills were an essential element of success for the small group of Afghan officers who had to act decisively and in concert to overcome the disadvantage of their numbers.

A second unusual aspect was Taraki's specific instruction concerning events that should be considered as adequate reason for triggering the coup:

> Should imperialism, reaction, or another group topple the Daoud Regime, the Democratic People's Party of Afghanistan should wrest the political power. In case the Daoud regime launched an offensive to incarcerate me (Comrade Taraki) in order to weaken or destroy the party members, the latter should commence the revolution to topple the Daoud Regime and wrest the political power.[3]

If this quote, unfortunately undated, was not made up after the fact, it provides a curiously specific set of circumstances—and only two of them at that—for "wresting the political power." It is almost as if Taraki had reason to anticipate a real or sham right-wing coup or his own arrest.

In this regard, another circumstance is even more significant. After the popular demonstrations that followed Mir Akbar Khyber's assassination, the midnight police sweep that resulted in Taraki's arrest and immediate incarceration also included the arrest of Amin and three other (unnamed) members of the PDPA Central Committee. Whereas Taraki was taken straight to jail, however, Amin was held under very loose house arrest for more than ten hours, from midnight to 10:45 A.M. on April 26. During this critical period he received visitors, sent his sons out to get information and to contact his Khalqi recruits in the military, and dispatched instructions to the latter on what each was to do—all without more than passing hindrance by his guards.

Finally (in the words of the PDPA), "At 10:30 A.M. on the twenty-sixth of April, work on planning and the revolution command was finalized and at 10:45 of the same day, three cars with armed policemen carried Comrade Amin to the jail, where he was delivered at exactly 11 A.M."[4]

Taraki had delegated to Amin the task of recruiting military officers into Khalq as early as 1973.[5] Of all the individuals for Daoud to have left essentially at large when a left-wing upheaval threatened, Amin was without doubt the most dangerous. The explanation for this fatal laxness may lie in the allegation by a former (1977) Daoud minister that Lieutenant Colonel Pacha Sarbaz, third in command of Afghan military counterintelligence just before the coup, was a Khalqi (and possibly Soviet) agent.[6] Any such person would doubtless have had advance warning of the arrests and might have had enough influence to arrange for a delay in Amin's removal to jail.

Or did the USSR have its own "moles" who helped to sabotage Daoud's arrest order and to coordinate the PDPA activities after arrests began cutting into PDPA ranks? Persistent reports of unusual activity at the Soviet Embassy in Kabul during the period of the coup are not proof of such involvement,[7] but do tend to discount Soviet Ambassador Puzanov's ingenuous statement, "no one was more surprised than I by the coup."[8]

As in 1973, there can be little doubt that the USSR was at least aware of the conspirators' coup plans; many of the Afghans were the same individuals who had brought Daoud to power. The intention, however, had been to act somewhat later, in August, as eventually stated by Taraki himself.[9] The coup was close to fruition anyway and only needed to be launched a few months earlier than originally anticipated.

An intriguing question is whether the triggering catalyst for the coup—Khyber's assassination—was a part of anyone's plans. From the Soviet and Parcham standpoint it surely was not, and to that extent Puzanov's statement can be taken at face value: he very likely expected events to unfold as they did, but in August, not April. Whether the Khalqis were caught unaware is less certain. In any case, it is interesting that almost from the outset of Taraki's rule the fact of Khyber's murder and its significance for the coup were ignored completely. The first full official report of the coup by the Taraki government does not even mention Khyber or the demonstrations surrounding his funeral march. Daoud's roundup of leftists is portrayed as an unprovoked police action.[10]

To the outside world, the coup came as a shock. Preliminary analysis in the West gave a picture of a beleaguered Afghan Left that staked all on a final, desperate throw of the dice to unseat Daoud. In the chaotic situation that developed, both loyalist and rebel forces made multiple errors and "the side with the fewer foul-ups won."[11]

In fact, however, there were remarkably few foul-ups on the part of the PDPA. Though extensive, PDPA penetrations of the military comprised only a small fraction of the officer corps, and though all of the party leadership had been in jail since April 26, the military penetrations acted with surprisingly good coordination. Amin's written instructions to them, composed and delivered between midnight and early morning on the twenty-sixth, provided a point of departure but were scarcely a substitute for ongoing leadership and command. By the time action commenced, on the morning of the twenty-seventh, the PDPA military officers were apparently on their own.

Amin's instructions had reportedly reached their recipients in *photocopy* form.[12] Bearing in mind that one can scarcely obtain photocopies commercially in Kabul in the best of circumstances, much less in the dawn hours, the implication is that diplomatic copying facilities were warmed up and waiting. Major Sayed Mohammed Gulabzoy, the individual responsible for delivering the instructions, had, as will be seen, close Soviet ties and would have known where to turn.[13] He appears to have served in a coordination, if not command, capacity once Amin was in jail.

Although there were communications failures and reported instances of inadvertent engagements between friendly forces, they were virtually unavoidable, for both sides used the same equipment and wore the same uniforms. It was safer for each individual to shoot first rather than wait for proper identification of friends or enemies.

The PDPA appeared to have penetrations in no fewer than twenty military units and airports.[14] Some of their officers were in key command positions; these included Majors Mohammed Aslam Watanjar, Sher Jan Mazdooryar, and Assadullah Payam in the Fourth Armored Division; and Lieutenant Colonel Abdul Qader who was chief of staff of the air force. Others held secondary ranks but were able to kill or incapacitate the pro-Daoud commanders and take charge themselves. This happened in the Thirty-Second Brigade, the Eighty-Eighth Anti-aircraft Artillery Unit, and in the Commandos. In the Seventh Division, the would-be PDPA commander, Mohammed Ali, was himself killed.[15]

The Republican Guard, the Fifteenth Armored Division, and the Seventh Division remained loyal and fought on behalf of Daoud. By the early morning hours of April 28, however, only the remnants of the Republican Guard still held out. It was the one unit that apparently had no reliable surviving PDPA penetrations. Until heavy losses forced surrender, it continued to defend the presidential palace where Daoud, his immediate family, and some close advisors had taken refuge.

They were all gathered in one room when a PDPA officer entered and demanded the Daoud surrender unconditionally. Instead, Daoud drew his pistol and opened fire. Others followed suit, and in the brief firefight that followed, Daoud and almost all of his family—including ten women and several children, the youngest of whom was three years old—were slain.[16]

The reign of the Mohammedzai family, extending almost unbroken back to the early nineteenth century, had ended; the long-term Soviet goal of establishing a pliable regime in Kabul had apparently been achieved.

On the part of both the Soviet Union and the newly established Democratic Republic of Afghanistan (DRA), however, there was a concentrated and partially successful effort to deny the fact that Afghanistan was now committed to the Soviet bloc. This effort was to continue into 1979, despite overwhelming evidence to the contrary, but it was particularly intense in the first days following the coup.[17] To describe the regime, terms such as "democratic, Islamic, reformist, and nonaligned,"[18] "progressive and patriotic,"[19] and (most hoary of all) "agrarian reformers"[20] were used by Afghan authorities, independent journalists, and even some Western students of the area who should have known better.

Another effort to downplay the significance of the coup was apparent in the deliberate Afghan understatement of casualties. Although the first Western reports almost surely exaggerated the bloodshed (initial reports were of ten thousand killed), the deaths unquestionably were in the thousands, not the "under one hundred" initially claimed by Taraki.[21] The two-thousand-strong Republican Guard, for example, fought until there were only some two hundred of them left, and when they finally surrendered, most were shot out of hand. A few were sent to Pul-e-Charki jail, but most of that group were also killed during the next few months in nightly executions by firing squad.[22]

Nonetheless, initial Afghan and Soviet propaganda was designed to convey the impression that the coup was a purely local phenomenon, an almost unopposed removal of a hated tyrant by a popular uprising that owed nothing to outside influence.

Although that picture is obviously distorted, the extent of Soviet influence is extremely difficult to measure, due to the secretiveness of both Afghan and Soviet sources. In the first months following the coup, Soviet influence did not amount to complete control, or the Parcham-Khalq conflict would not have been allowed to split the PDPA anew. On the other hand, it was pervasive, as indicated by an oblique reference made by Taraki to the Central Committee Historical Commission in November 1978. Following a description of the organization of party commissions and duties of party secretaries in managing state and party affairs, he said,

> This has been organized on the basis of profound studies and specialized advices [sic]. During the first days of the Revolution some persons who had specialization in Party organization came to Kabul at the invitation of the Secretariat of the Party and studied for three months Party affairs here and consequently they gave specialized advice to the Party and it was on the basis of these advices that the Party is always organized.[23]

Although Taraki did not name the nationality of the advisors, there can be little doubt that they came from the USSR. The task apparently was to help the PDPA in the difficult transition stage from its role as a conspiratorial underground opposition to that of a ruling party.

In the first PDPA cabinet, announced on May 1, 1978, the strength of Parcham and Khalq seemed to have been carefully balanced by assigning ministries in order of importance first to one faction and then to the other. In fact, although the Khalqis held the nominally top positions of prime minister (Nur Mohammed Taraki) and minister of foreign affairs (Hafizullah Amin), Parcham appeared to control the ministries of defense, interior, and communications. Of these latter, the Ministry of Defense is the ultimate source of political power in the country, while the Ministry of Interior and Ministry of Communications have high strategic importance as well. Inasmuch as Parcham had always had the reputation of being slightly favored over Khalq by the Soviets, the apparent Parcham upper hand was not surprising.

The Parchami minister of defense, Abdul Qader, however, though a hero of the revolution, was no politician. As noted above, he had helped Daoud come to power in 1973, and had been elevated to the position of air force chief of staff; but he then had criticized Daoud for moving too slowly toward socialism and had been demoted promptly to officer in charge of military slaughterhouses. Later reinstated to his former position by Daoud, he led the air force against his mentor, playing a key role in the 1978 coup.[24]

The PDPA figure who had the closest connections with the military was a Khalqi, Hafizullah Amin. It was he who had recruited most of the military cadres for Khalq, and who had done the organizational work for the coup among the military. He was also a politician at heart, and would not have been likely to relinquish his military contacts after the coup had succeeded. In fact, on being released from jail the evening of April 27, "Comrade Amin introduced other Central Committee members to the revolutionary officers."[25] The implication is that up until that time, both Khalqi and Parchami penetrations of the military had been compartmented even from other Central Committee members, who had communicated with them only through Amin. Thus, though Parcham was also represented in the military, and a Parchami was minister of defense, it is probable that Khalq had the dominant influence in the armed forces.

Furthermore, although the Ministry of Interior was in the hands of a loyal Parchami (Nur Ahmad Nur), the reputedly Parchami-oriented minister of communications (Aslam Watanjar) successfully converted to Khalq when the Parchamis were purged.

Through May and the first week in June, there were few outward manifestations of the struggle for control of the PDPA that must have been going on between Khalqis and Parchamis. In the pages of the *Kabul Times*, pictures of Parcham leaders appeared as often as those of Khalqis. On May 22, however, the Political Department of the Armed Forces of Afghanistan published a pamphlet ("On the Saur Revolution") that avoided all mention of such Parcham figures as Babrak and Anahita Ratebzad, although it paid due respect to such pro-Parcham military officers as Qader. (The effusive praise heaped on Amin in this publication was a good indication of the influence that he continued to wield in the military.)

In the middle of June, there was, in the *Kabul Times*, a sudden cessation of photos of PDPA leaders, Parcham and Khalq alike. The last photo before this blackout was on June 8, when Babrak was featured warmly welcoming Amin back from a visit abroad. In late June, pictures of Amin and Taraki began to appear again—at the same time that foreign postings of ranking Parchamis also began to be announced.

Although Khalq thus declared subtly that it had won the first round for control of the party, the struggle itself appeared to have been conducted in a relatively civilized manner. The losers, in line with precommunist Afghan tradition, were sent abroad into honorable, ambassadorial exile.

Following the announcement of the departure of the principal Parchamis in early July, the personality cult that had been building up around Taraki ever since the coup became more apparent, recalling the days of Stalin. On July 25 he was referred to as "Great Leader" in the *Kabul Times*, and this sobriquet soon appeared in almost every news story that mentioned his name—a large percentage of the stories printed at that time. Virtually every indoors photograph showing any Afghan official other than Taraki himself managed to include in it a portrait of Great Leader. (The definite article was usually omitted in the headlines, lending an even more Stalinist aspect to the coverage.) By early August the portraits on the wall (obviously dubbed into the photographs) were dwarfing the ministers conducting business under their benign gaze.[26] The portraits also tended to be more in focus than the faces of the ministers, which over time seemed to become ever smaller and more fuzzily anonymous.

On August 17, the regime announced the arrest of General Abdul Qader for plotting against it.[27] Other arrests followed, including that of the ministers of public works (Lt. Col. Mohammed Rafiee) and of planning (Sultan Ali Kishtmand). Only a month later did the extent of the purported plot emerge, as the government newspapers devoted entire oversize editions on September 23 to the confessions of the conspirators.[28]

The Afghan media were at first apparently hesitant to heap too much ideological abuse on Babrak and the other exiled Parchamis who were also implicated in the conspiracy. The plotters reportedly intended to follow the same foreign and domestic policies as the existing regime, but under a renamed *People's* Democratic Republic of Afghanistan. Relying on "national progressive forces," the conspirators promised to share power with the Khalqis if the latter would agree to cooperate. The coup was scheduled for August, during the Eid festival that marks the end of the Ramadan fast. (This was, by the way, the time originally set by the PDPA for the coup against Daoud.) The Parchamis abroad would return to Kabul unannounced via Iran and Pakistan to lead the coup. The motive for the coup was given as the frustrated personal ambitions of Babrak and others who had been shunted aside by the Khalqis.[29]

All of this is fairly straightforward and probably accurate. Far harder to clarify are the murky allegations by the Afghan press concerning the involvement of foreign powers in the plot. Evidence for such involvement was claimed "on the basis of undeniable documents," yet nowhere is there a hint of the countries involved. The foreign linkage was allegedly via unspecified "elements attached to reaction and imperialism"[30]—yet the foreign powers were said also to have a "political accord" with the plotters that the latter should continue the Afghan policy of "positive and active nonalignment"—a standard euphemism for an ostensibly neutral but firmly pro-Soviet orientation.

It seemed bizarre at the time that the USSR might be involved in toppling the regime of its own client state, a hypothesis that only became undeniably credible when, fifteen months later, Babrak was returned to power by an invading Soviet army. Nevertheless, even in 1978 the USSR had reason to be dismayed with the course of events in Afghanistan. Worse, from the Kremlin's standpoint, its power to dictate corrective measures to the regime in power was circumscribed to some degree.

As long as Parcham and Khalq had been in quasi-legal opposition to the Afghan government, the USSR had had leverage to force them into mending their differences. Once the reunited PDPA succeeded in "wresting the political power" from Daoud in April 1978, however, it gained a greater measure of independence from the USSR, especially in the conduct of its internal affairs. Inasmuch as both Khalq and Parcham factions were apparently equally pro-Soviet, Moscow at first seems to have assumed that it did not matter very much which faction emerged victorious in their own internal struggle. There was probably some hope that the two in fact could reach a lasting compromise, and if they could not, Moscow was then prepared to go along with whichever faction triumphed. A few leaders might be deposed, jailed, or even executed, but in the end the party would emerge the stronger for having purged itself of leadership elements personally unable to accommodate to the winners.

The USSR overlooked (and apparently has continued to overlook) the depth of hostility that Afghan enemies (especially Pashtuns) develop against each other as a matter of course. The term *feudal* has a meaning that extends beyond economics, and Afghanistan is especially feudal when it comes to loyalties and antagonisms. The Pashtunwali, the Pashtun code of conduct, which tradition demands be memorized by all Pashtun youths, sets forth the rules governing blood feuds as a first order of business. Such feuds know no bounds in time or space, and the exacting of vengeance is supposed to be a priority matter for every wronged individual or (if he is killed) for his appropriate surviving male relative, whether or not the latter was personally wronged.

The hostilities that developed between Parcham and Khalq from 1967 to 1977 were far too fundamental to be reconciled by one year of enforced cooperation. The antagonism did not exist merely at the top level, but extended down to the rank and file as well. No matter that the two factions, even when combined, were still only a tiny minority of the population (only a few thousand out of perhaps fifteen to seventeen million), and that excommunication of one or the other from the PDPA would imperil the very survival of the party. Vengeance was more important, and the Khalqis lost no time in exacting it. As soon as it became apparent that the Parcham leadership had lost in the struggle with Khalq, Parchamis at all levels were hounded, imprisoned, and often shot. (Had Parcham emerged the victor, there might have been somewhat less violent a reaction—Parcham was less Pashtun-oriented than Khalq, though it still had a significant Pashtun membership—but some degree of violence would have been inevitable. As experience in 1980 has shown, Khalqi losers are no less bloodthirsty than Khalqi winners, and the feud would have erupted in any case.)

Despite the still tenuous hold that Taraki had on the country, by eliminating the Parchamis he and his followers had cut their meager support by nearly half. Furthermore, free of the somewhat moderating Parchami influence, the regime undertook policies that were less and less acceptable to the Afghan population at large. Daoud's exile of the 160 Parchami reformers into the countryside as sub-governors had given Parcham a hands-on experience in rural administration not shared by the Khalqi leaders, even though most Khalqis were country bred. Having tried—and failed—to impose reforms from above in the countryside, the Parchamis doubtless counseled caution to Khalqi colleagues, advice that was ignored once the Parchami leaders were deposed.

Khalqi insensitivity to public opinion continued to be illustrated after the Parcham coup failed. On October 19, after preliminary publicity that should have provided a chance for opponents to voice objections, Taraki personally raised Afghanistan's new national banner—a blood-red, close copy of the Soviet flag. His elimination of Islamic green from the national standard was one of the most foolish of his many provocative moves against Afghan tradition. In 1980, Babrak was to restore a version of the old flag in a belated and unsuccessful attempt to regain public confidence.

From the Soviet standpoint, Taraki's negative impact in the countryside was a serious matter. Immediately after the coup (and sporadically at later dates), the Kabul regime appeared to be trying to revive the Pashtunistan issue.[31] Even more than in the case of predecessor regimes, the USSR had reason for wishing Taraki success in this effort. With a firmly pro-Soviet regime in power in Kabul, instability to the south and west opened up ever greater opportunities for Soviet interference and ultimate control in those regions as well. Many in the West had forebodings of just such a development.[32]

Far from establishing a base for spreading unrest among Pashtuns on the other side of the border, however, Taraki's policies from the outset alienated his own Pashtun population to an ever greater extent. Rural resentment had already become resistance; resistance was becoming rebellion;[33] and rebellion showed signs of becoming a *jihad*, a holy war against the infidel Kabul regime. Instead of being an exporter of instability, Afghanistan showed signs of becoming an unwilling importer as refugees from the Khalqis flowed into Pakistan, established their own settlements, and set up lines of communication back into their homeland.

As a result of all this, the USSR had cause to support Babrak covertly in 1978, just as later, in 1979, they supported him openly with their armed forces. Babrak could be counted on to pursue more sophisticated, less abrasive policies toward the population than Taraki. On the other hand, in 1978 the Soviets were still attempting to preserve the fiction of their noninvolvement in Afghan internal affairs. Unless and until Babrak were securely in power in Kabul, the USSR would be risking serious embarrassment by aiding him; great pains would have been taken to conceal any such involvement.

If the USSR was in fact supporting Babrak, did the Khalqis detect that fact? It seems not, although as indicated above they appeared to be convinced that *some* foreign power was involved. In the days following the September 23 exposé, Kabul newspapers were more than usually effusive in praise for the USSR; they were also careful to replay Soviet praise for the Taraki regime.[34] At the same time however, at least one ranking bloc diplomat left Kabul under unexplained circumstances. Hermann Schwiessau, ambassador from the German Democratic Republic, presented his credentials on August 8, 1978, yet departed permanently and without any newspaper coverage some time during the next few months. He was to be replaced, probably in early 1979, by one Kraft Bumbel, whose arrival went similarly unannounced.

The Soviet ambassador, Puzanov, remained at his post. A year later, after involving himself more directly in Afghan internal politics, he was indeed asked to leave, but in 1978 there was no evidence of Afghan displeasure with him or his country.

Whether or not the USSR had tried to aid Babrak, it appeared to decide at this point to accommodate itself more thoroughly to the Khalqi regime. In fact, relations seemed to move ahead significantly. In November the Afghan ambassador in Moscow was quoted as having declared that Afghan-Soviet relations were now changing from friendship to fraternity. Challenged with defining the meaning of this change, Amin insisted that despite some parallels with Soviet policy Afghanistan was still following a "strict policy of nonalignment."[35] It was not a convincing statement.

At the same time, the USSR may have been successful in persuading Taraki to take a softer line internally. Although the decision on the new Soviet-style flag was not rescinded (it would have represented too sharp a retreat), in late October the regime released from jail seventy-three women and children belonging to the former ruling family.[36] They were given the option of remaining in Afghanistan and working for the new regime, or emigrating permanently. Inasmuch as their property and possessions had been confiscated, most chose to emigrate. Their release was a surprisingly lenient move for the hard-line Khalqis to make.

Perhaps even more surprising was the continued survival of General Abdul Qader and Sultan Ali Kishtmand. It is the practice of most communist states to mete out justice, especially capital punishment, without delay. Afghanistan has been no exception in this regard (nor was it before the Communists took over, for that matter), yet Qader's death sentence for his part in the anti-Khalq conspiracy was never carried out. One can only assume that there was significant pressure from some quarter (most logically the USSR) to stay the execution. The following year, in October 1979, Amin commuted Qader's sentence to fifteen years imprisonment, possibly as a further placating gesture toward the USSR.

On December 5, 1978, the Afghans signed a Friendship Agreement with the USSR in Moscow. The provisions of the treaty, including Article IV which stipulated that the signatories "shall consult with each other and take by agreement appropriate measures to ensure the security, independence, and territorial integrity of the two countries," indeed signaled a closer relationship.[37] Furthermore, as noted by some Western observers, similar friendship treaties signed by India (1971) and Vietnam (1978) had been the immediate precursors of armed hostilities by those two countries against their neighbors: India's invasion of East Pakistan (thereafter Bangladesh) and Vietnam's invasion of Cambodia.[38] Although it seemed clear that Afghanistan at that time was not in a position to invade anybody, there was an obvious need for more Soviet arms and advisors just to keep the country from falling to the insurgents.

In February 1979 the ability of the United States to influence events in the country received a severe setback with the tragic abduction and murder of U. S. Ambassador Adolph Dubs in downtown Kabul. Although there were American, Afghan, and Soviet officials who were all but eyewitnesses to the crime, it has never been satisfactorily explained. Briefly, four men, one in a policeman's uniform, hijacked the ambassador's limousine (within plain sight of at least one real Afghan policeman) and took their victim to a nearby hotel. There, demands were allegedly made that the DRA release one or more religious or political prisoners. No demands were made of the American government, nor did the DRA ever give a complete or consistent version of the kidnappers' desires. After four hours, police under visible direction of Soviet officials, despite the protests of American diplomats on the spot, opened fire and stormed the hotel room. The ambassador and two kidnappers died in the 40-second firefight that ensued; the bodies of the other two, taken alive but apparently shot shortly thereafter, were shown to American officials before sundown.

Subsequently, several communist versions of the incident, each more outlandish than the last and all designed to incriminate the CIA, Amin, or both, surfaced in the Soviet and Afghan media. Despite these efforts, it was obvious there was only one power that would benefit from the murder—the Soviet Union. The relations that the United States and its ambassador had tried with such patience to maintain with the DRA were irrevocably poisoned, leaving the USSR with a monopoly of great power influence over the Taraki government.[39]

Meantime, Soviet arms continued to be delivered to Afghanistan, but without any appreciable effect on government success in stamping out rebel activities. Instead of intimidating the resistance, the new levels of Soviet military aid seemed to inflame it. In March 1979 the city of Herat in western Afghanistan was engulfed by a spontaneous rebellion that saw some forty Soviet advisors and dependents massacred by the population. Overall Soviet deaths in clashes with insurgents were estimated at one hundred for the month.[40]

Possibly in response to this heightened violence, Taraki turned over the position of premier to Amin at the end of March. Taraki retained the positions of both defense minister and head of state, but Amin's new authority was thought to herald both firmer measures against the Muslim insurgents and closer Afghan ties to Moscow. Amin was believed to be "a hardline communist . . . even more servile to the Soviet Union than President Taraki."[41] At the same time, Soviet arms aid to Afghanistan was reported to have increased.[42]

The arms aid was followed immediately by a visit to Afghanistan by a Soviet military team headed by General Aleksey Alekseyevich Yepishev. Yepishev, who had played a major role in the 1968 Soviet occupation of Czechoslovakia, was one of the highest ranking Soviet officers to go to Afghanistan, and his visit was taken as a reflection of the seriousness of the problems facing the Afghan army in attempting to put down the Muslim insurgents.[43]

Although the news took months to seep out to the West, Yepishev's visit coincided with the deliberate massacre of the entire male population of the village of Kerala, northeast of Kabul. Over eleven hundred people were shot by Afghan troops and police under the direct command of Soviet advisors because the village was suspected (with good reason) of having supported the insurgents.[44] This mass execution did not deter the resistance, which only multiplied its attacks on government installations.

As the year advanced, the Kabul government's inability to deal with the insurgency became more and more apparent. In early August, a mutiny inside Kabul's Bala Hissar fortress had to be put down with helicopter gunships and tanks, in a battle that lasted for four hours.[45] A week later, an entire Afghan armored brigade went over to the insurgents taking its equipment with it.[46]

At this point Afghanistan recieved a visit by another prestigious Soviet military figure, General Ivan G. Pavlovskiy, commanding general of all Soviet ground forces. Pavlovskiy arrived in mid-August, with an entourage of fifty officers, and stayed for nearly two months. [47] His visit was not announced in the Kabul press and only later came to light in the West. [48]

In spite (or perhaps because) of the deteriorating security situation and the presence of a ranking Soviet general, President Taraki left on September 1 for the Non-Aligned Nations' Conference in Havana. His route, going and returning, lay via the USSR, and he stopped over briefly in Moscow on both legs of his journey. The details of his discussions there are a Kremlin secret, but it was credibly reported that the USSR successfully pressured him into reconciling his differences with Babrak and laying plans for a renewed Parcham-Khalq coalition government. [49] It was also reported that, while in Moscow, Taraki met with Babrak to seal the bargain. [50]

To explain the sudden rehabilitation of Babrak, who had been excoriated in the Afghan press as a vile traitor, it was necessary to find some new villain whose alleged false witness had misled Taraki concerning Babrak. Such a scapegoat could also be held responsible for all else that had gone wrong in Afghanistan over the past eighteen months. Only one person met all the qualifications: Hafizullah Amin. [51]

It should have been abundantly clear to Moscow that even liquidation of Amin and a Parcham-Khalq reconciliation would not be sufficient to stem the insurgency. The only chance to pacify the country lay in Soviet military intervention. One can postulate, therefore, that Taraki returned to Afghanistan with a plan not only to denounce, arrest, and execute Amin (possibly on the grounds of the same accusation that was to appear later—that Amin was a CIA agent) and to effect a public reconciliation with Babrak, but also to announce jointly with him an invitation for active Soviet participation (i.e., combat troops) to dispose of the insurgency. Both the continued presence in Afghanistan of the large Pavlovskiy military delegation and a sudden upsurge in Soviet military activity near the Afghan border in mid-September lend credence to this hypothesis. [52]

Taraki returned to Kabul on September 11 and reported immediately to the cabinet. During his absence, there had been no diminution of his personality cult in the Afghan media. From September 2 through September 12, the front-page lead headline in every issue of the *Kabul*

Times referred in one context or another to "Great Leader." On September 13, this practice suddenly came to a permanent halt. September 14 was a Friday, the Muslim sabbath, so no newspaper appeared. The next (September 15) issue featured front-page coverage of a news conference Taraki had held in Havana, but this clearly represented an *ad hoc* insertion of dated material by editors who must have been puzzled by the absence of copy on their most consistent news subject. By that time, unknown to any but Amin's inner circle, Taraki was already under arrest.

On September 16 all of Taraki's titles were assumed by Amin. Almost as a footnote, it was announced that the Plenum of the Central Committee had approved Taraki's request to be relieved of his duties "in view of my bad health and nervous weakness."[53]

On September 12, between Taraki's return and his "resignation," the *Kabul Times* carried belated coverage of an Amin news conference held three days earlier. During the conference Amin vigorously denied that the major military airbase at Bagram (near Kabul) had been turned over to the USSR, declared that Soviet troops were not involved in fighting insurgents and would not be so involved in the future, and asserted that Afghanistan had no intention of joining the Warsaw Pact.[54] Previous reports in the Western media had indeed claimed that such measures were being undertaken or were in the offing. Amin's denials were therefore not completely unprovoked. Nevertheless, their timing and vehemence probably represent his first steps to thwart Taraki's plans to deliver the country into Soviet hands and make Amin a scapegoat.

Amin did not confine himself to words. He swiftly dismissed from his cabinet three key members also involved in the plot: Minister of Interior Watanjar (shifted six weeks earlier from his even more strategic position of minister of defense, which was assumed by Amin), Minister of Communications Gulabzoy, and Minister of Frontier Affairs Mazdooryar (a former minister of interior who was shifted to frontier affairs when Watanjar took over interior).

All three of these men had been instrumental in bringing Daoud to power in 1973; all had played key roles in the 1978 coup that toppled him; and all, although originally Parchamis, had survived Babrak's downfall in 1978 by switching their allegiance to Khalq. Furthermore, all three were to make yet another apparent reversal by rejoining Babrak as cabinet members in January 1980, following the Soviet invasion. In the interim, despite protests by Amin and his foreign minister, Shah Wali, they were given asylum in the Soviet Embassy in Kabul.[55] In retrospect, it seems most probable that the primary loyalties of the three were less to any Afghan political faction or personality than to the USSR.

Apparently Amin acted swiftly to neutralize Watanjar, Gulabzoy, and Mazdooryar as soon as he became aware of the plot against him. His informant in this case was almost surely his chief of security, Major Sayed Daoud Taroon, who had accompanied Taraki throughout his trip to Havana, and who therefore was probably involved in (or became aware of) the Moscow discussions on removing his chief.

On September 14, Taraki telephoned Amin and summoned him to the presidential palace. Amin must have been reluctant to go, for it was necessary for Soviet ambassador Puzanov, who was present with Taraki, to take up the telephone and assure Amin of safe conduct. Amin then agreed to come, but he was obviously still suspicious, for he and his escort, including Major Taroon, were all armed. As they entered the building, they fell into an ambush, and at least four of the escort, including Taroon, were killed. Amin, however, fought his way clear and survived unscathed.[56]

The failed ambush sealed Taraki's fate. With the key ministries of defense, interior, and communications lost to him, there was no possibility of staging a coup against Amin. Taraki's only chance for survival would have lain in making his way to the Soviet Embassy to join his three ex-ministers, but Amin must have reckoned with this possibility and lost no time in having Taraki arrested.

Amin's government never did reveal Taraki's arrest, but the following day, September 15, it announced the appointment of new ministers to the posts previously held by Watanjar, Gulabzoy, and Mazdooryar.[57] Gunfire and explosions were heard in Kabul immediately thereafter, apparently indicating that these personnel decisions were being vigorously, if unsuccessfully, disputed. Those opposed to the government's action were subsequently referred to as "some enemies of the people [who] have been eliminated."[58]

On September 16 the *Kabul Times* announced Taraki's retirement from the political scene and Amin's takeover of Taraki's responsibilities. It also reported Taroon's September 14 "martyrdom" and subsequent burial with full honors. On September 18, the other three known "martyrs" were also identified. They were: Nawab (deputy chief of intelligence), engineer Khair Mohammed (president of the "Afghan Construction Unit"), and—conceivably accompanying Amin in anticipation of the need for swift medical treatment for a variety of assassination techniques—Dr. Sur Gul Khataz (president of preventive medicine in the Ministry of Public Health).

That same day Ambassador Puzanov, in what must be one of the most flagrant recorded instances of diplomatic hypocrisy, publicly signed the condolence book for Taroon.[59] On September 19, Brezhnev and Kosygin sent their congratulations to Amin, and the latter's triumph appeared to be complete.[60]

Following the announcement of his resignation, Taraki's name was eclipsed from the Afghan media. There was to be only one exception. On October 10, the *Kabul Times* carried the following article (quoted here in full) on its final page, near the bottom:

TARAKI DIES OF ILLNESS

Kabul Oct 10 (Bakhtiar)—Noor Mohammed Taraki, former President of the Revolutionary Council, died yesterday morning of serious illness, which he had been suffering for some time.

The body of the deceased was buried in his family graveyard yesterday.

That was the total obituary coverage of a man whose titles alone had taken almost as many lines in news stories until three weeks before the announcement of his death.

The second Afghan leader in eighteen months had died violently at the hands of his successor. The third had less than three months to live before suffering the same fate.

CHAPTER
8

Prelude to Invasion
September–December 1979

One can rarely see neighborliness without some clashes, tensions, and misunderstanding. However, in connection with the DRA and USSR such things have never happened and we are sure that they will never happen in the future . . . Of course the main and important reason behind this friendship and mutual understanding lies in the fact that the two nations have the greatest respect to vital principles of good relation between nations which are respect to independence, sovereignty, territorial integrity and mutual cooperation without any conditions and strings. . . .

(*Kabul Times* editorial "DRA-USSR friendship treaty," December 6, 1979.)

If the reported date of Taraki's death (the night of October 8–9) is accurate, it had taken Amin three weeks to reach the decision to do away with his rival. During this time he had had to weigh a number of factors: (1) Soviet complicity in the abortive ambush against him and the Soviets' clear preference for Taraki over him; (2) Soviet denial of any knowledge of the whereabouts of Watanjar, Mazdooryar, and Gulabzoy, all of whom were known (or at least strongly presumed) to be sheltered in the Soviet Embassy; and (3) the continued presence in Afghanistan of the large military delegation under Pavlovskiy. Amin had to reckon with the danger that the liquidation of Taraki might provoke the Soviets into taking decisive action against him. On the other hand, he could scarcely afford to let the former "Great Leader" remain alive and perhaps become the nucleus of a new opposition to his rule.

In 1980 Taraki's murder, by strangulation and suffocation, was described in grisly detail in the published confessions of Amin's lieutenants.[1] This seems convincing refutation of earlier reports in Western media that he had died of gunshot wounds received in the shoot-out.[2]

The congratulatory telegrams on his accession to power that poured in from almost all Soviet bloc chiefs of state during the last part of September probably contributed to Amin's confidence.[3] So, in all likelihood, did the fact that the USSR itself signed various aid and trade agreements during this period and into October.[4] And, perhaps most significant of all to Amin, the Pavlovskiy delegation finally completed its visit and returned to the USSR.[5]

Whatever Amin's considerations, he disposed of his rival with a minimum of fanfare and appeared to emerge the clear victor. Nonetheless, his position was not an enviable one. Only about half of his army's normal officer corps strength of eight thousand remained; the rest had been killed or had gone over to the rebels. Mutinies in his forces had become commonplace. The PDPA, splintered by the excommunication of the Parchamis in 1978, was now splitting again as Amin's supporters ranged against those of Taraki. Insurgency was everywhere; the government could control individual cities by dispatching its dwindling military forces to the most critical danger points, but not even Kabul was safe from insurgent attacks and military rebellions. Afghanistan's economy was in a shambles. And looming over other considerations was the all-too-evident military solution that the USSR might seek to impose if the Afghans failed to set their own house in order.

Amin's response to this situation was to placate as many of his immediate and potential enemies as he could without at the same time weakening his political position by making real concessions. To mollify the Soviets, he commuted the still-pending death sentences of Kishtmand and Qader to fifteen years imprisonment, and he kept up a steady drumfire of pro-Soviet propaganda in the official Afghan media. His relations with the USSR, he was to tell an American historian in November, were "based on profound ideological roots."[6] In anticipation of the Soviet National Day (November 7), the *Kabul Times* again referred to Afghanistan's role as a "continuation of the Great October Revolution."[7]

For his domestic audience, propaganda during October and November addressed both internal and external problems in about equal measure without ever quite admitting that they existed. The messages were aimed primarily at dampening the insurgency.

There were periodic reports of the release of hundreds of prisoners from various jails in various parts of the country. (This had been an intermittent propaganda theme since the summer of 1978, and Amin revived it.) Such reports never gave the names of those released or the crimes for which they had been arrested; but the overall impression was one of jails being emptied of all their inmates, who now no longer posed a threat to society.[8]

Claims were made that the government was in favor of "complete freedom of religion and profound respect to Islam and a widescale support thereto," but these claims were accompanied by demands that "religious fanaticism" be wiped out.[9]

Amnesty was offered for those who had "abandoned their homeland" (i.e., fled to Pakistan or Iran); these offers were accompanied by interviews with happy returnees.[10]

There were, however, some jarring notes as well, particularly as Amin's position vis-à-vis the insurgency continued to deteriorate. In November and December there was a spate of articles dealing with the "voluntary" requests for extension of service by individual soldiers and whole units, to "defend the revolution" or to "fight bandits."[11]

In addition, there was one article that highlighted a heretofore largely unpublicized collectivization effort.[12] This was a drive that could not have been at all popular among Afghanistan's individualistic farmers, many of whose fathers had fled collectivization in Soviet Central Asia. The November 6 timing of this article may indicate that it was intended more to impress Afghanistan's Soviet mentors on the eve of the October Revolution holiday than any domestic audience.

Although there was no interruption in the stream of panegyrics offered up to the Soviet Union, most notably on November 7 but also at other times,[13] a close observer would have noted that only Foreign Minister Shah Wali, not Hafizullah Amin, attended the National Day ceremonies at the Soviet Embassy. Ambassador Puzanov was still in place, and Amin had reason to treat his invitations with some circumspection. (On November 22, Puzanov left Afghanistan permanently, allegedly in compliance with Amin's complaint concerning his September activities.)[14]

Similarly, in an exchange of telegrams on the occasion of the first anniversary of the Soviet-Afghan Friendship Treaty (December 5,

1979), Amin's congratulations went personally to Brezhnev and Kosygin, while their telegram, though addressed to Amin, sent greetings to the "Central Committee, Revolutionary Council, and government of the DRA," but not to Amin personally.[15]

Despite the concentration of lavish praise on the USSR, there began to appear on the back page of the *Kabul Times* a slow but perhaps significant trickle of articles concerning aid donations by the West. Such aid had never ceased entirely, even during 1978: the Afghans had no reason to turn down unencumbered donations, and the West wanted to keep alive at least an implicit Afghan debt of gratitude.

Some of the aid did not seem to serve the West's best interests. For example, a September 1978 DM 1,000,000 grant-in-aid to the Afghan Ministry of Interior from the Federal Republic of Germany was described as being intended for "technical affairs." The Afghan signatory was Major Taroon, the security chief, who had a reputation for torturing prisoners and who was to die at Amin's side a year later in the shootout with Taraki's backers. The funds were used to support and equip Taroon's secret police, whose avowed task was to protect the revolution at all costs.

Other grants, however, had humanitarian impact. The Saudis, for example, had extended $5,000,000 for flood relief in September 1978; the following month a 1977 West German DM 45,000,000 loan for economic development and medical aid was changed to a grant-in-aid.[16]

In October 1979 the *Kabul Times* contained articles on the delivery of a DC-10 to Ariana Afghan Airlines and on a U.S. AID grant.[17] In November there were stories (some accompanied by photos) about American chargé d'affaires Bruce Amstutz giving a $109,844 check to Minister of Education Mohammed Salem Masoodi for use on school buildings, the British ambassador presenting a donation of books, the U.S. sale of cotton ginning equipment, and other similar stories.[18] All such stories continued to appear on the back page, however.

In November there was even a hint that Amin might want to mend relations with Iran. In contrast to his anti-Khomeini propaganda in October, Amin told an American interviewer he was "looking forward to removal of all misunderstandings" between the countries.[19]

Another noticeable feature of the Afghan press, as autumn turned toward winter, was the growth of Amin's own personality cult.

Although he did not assume the "Great Leader" title assumed by Taraki, and although articles decrying the latter's cult (without ever mentioning his name) were common,[20] Amin's cult offered, if anything, a more flagrant warping of reality than his predecessor's. The same practice of including all of his party and state titles at the first mention of his name was a carry-over from Taraki, and Amin's was now the ubiquitous portrait that was shown suspended on every official's wall. He injected a new dimension in cult photography, however: the selective enlargement of his head when he was portrayed in a group. At first only slightly noticeable, the differential in size between him and those with whom he was conferring gradually became grotesque, with the ultimate effect of making him seem a giant among pygmies.[21]

By the end of November Amin's situation was critical, even though he appeared to have fought his internal enemies (excluding the anticommunist insurgents) to a standstill. In mid-October he had survived a coup attempt that seemed to combine the forces of the extreme political right and those of the ousted pro-Soviet left. The latter were represented by an army unit, loyal to Major Watanjar, that was stationed near Kabul and that attempted to mutiny on October 14 or 15.[22]

The political right was the "Afghan Mellat," a political party that dated from the 1960s and promoted national democratic socialism. Although ostensibly in favor of constitutional monarchy at that time, the main planks of its platform—racially oriented nationalism, jingoistic territorial ambitions (it wished to restore Afghanistan to its eighteenth-century borders), and implacable hatred for the West—had more in common with Nazi doctrine than with democracy. It reportedly attempted a coup at the same time as the army unit, and in about the same area. Amin arrested its leaders, the seventy-five-year-old Ghulam Mohammed Farhad and his immediate male relatives, including Qudratullah Haddad, the former editor of the Afghan Mellat's journal, also called *Afghan Mellat.*[23]

It is perhaps tempting to see in the highly chauvinistic, virulently anti-American *Afghan Mellat* an organ that was secretly under Soviet control in the years before Daoud suppressed all private press activity. It would not be the first example of Soviet manipulation of ostensibly far-right organs to promote communist goals. According to one former Afghan government official, however, Ghulam Mohammed Farhad concentrated his published xenophobia on the United States because it was a safer target than the USSR. He detested the USSR with even greater vigor, but dared not say so except in private, because of the proximity of the USSR and the influence wielded by leftist groups in Afghanistan.[24]

Why were the Soviets so bent on removing Amin? They have never admitted complicity in his removal in the first place, but have supported Babrak's accusations, which range from the hypocritical to the absurd, e.g., that Amin was cruel, that he was an agent of the CIA, and that he was trying to strike some kind of bargain with the Pakistanis. Of these, only the first is undeniable. The second is patently false, and the third is open to question.

Amin's most grievous sin in Soviet eyes may have been a refusal to accede to demands that he issue a formal invitation for the full-fledged invasion that followed. Earlier in the autumn he appears to have asked for truly "limited contingents" of Soviet troops to quell the resistance, but he wished these to be under Afghan command or, at worst, under joint Soviet-Afghan command. Neither condition would have been acceptable to the Soviets, who, however, could scarcely have overlooked the desirability, indeed the political necessity, for a bona fide invitation to legitimize their action. The difference between an intervention that has been sanctioned and even requested by a chief of state, and one that must be extended ex post facto by a successor whom the intervening force brings with it is the difference between true fraternal assistance and outright military invasion. Convincing Amin of the need for such an invitation would be no easy task—the memories of the September ambush were still fresh in his mind—but the deteriorating security situation for the DRA meant that some action had to be taken if the entire Soviet investment in the country were not to be sacrificed.

Contrary to what many analysts (including this one) have concluded in the past, the Soviet decision to invade in December 1979 does *not* appear to have derived from an ideological imperative based on the Brezhnev Doctrine. This common misapprehension has been justified chiefly on the basis of several statements during the first half of 1979 by authoritative Soviet sources who implied Afghanistan was part of the socialist commonwealth.[25] As such, the country would have been subject to occupation under the same terms as Czechoslovakia in 1968, i.e., the self-assigned obligation of the USSR for the armed defense of socialism "wherever in the world it might be threatened."

Such an analysis overlooks the fact that after mid-1979 the "socialist" label for Afghanistan vanished from Soviet pronouncements, and, following the invasion, from official Afghan commentary as well. Instead, since early 1980 Soviet and Afghan ideologues have gone to considerable pains to emphasize that the country is in the "national democratic" phase of development, and the Soviet occupation is justified only on the basis of state-to-state, not ideological, relations.[26] The point is worth emphasizing, because it bears on the degree of Soviet commitment to keep its troops in the country indefinitely. The absence of a socialist designation of Afghanistan means that whatever other considerations might influence Soviet behavior, at least there are no ideological barriers to an eventual withdrawal.

When it came, however, the Soviet invasion was no less massive for want of ideological underpinnings. Commitment of troops on the scale employed in late December is not something that one improvises on short notice. There was unusual military activity in connection with the invasion as early as October and November, when small units of Soviet Central Asian troops began taking over some guard functions from Afghan forces along critical communications links. This was done ostensibly to free Afghan troops for combat with the insurgents, but the real purpose was to control vital invasion routes.[27]

In late November, Soviet troops were put in a state of limited readiness, and reservists were called up to fill out understrength combat divisions in the Central Asian Military District. Bridging equipment was moved to the Afghan border; Marshal Sergey L. Sokolov set up his headquarters at Termez, just over the border from Afghanistan; and the Warsaw Pact countries placed their forces on an advanced state of readiness.[28]

About mid-December, the Soviets airlifted one or two battalions of troops with heavy weapons (armor and artillery) into Bagram Air Base, whose management (despite Amin's earlier denials) they had been steadily usurping from the Afghans over the preceding months. None of the above provoked any known U.S. protest. As noted subsequently by one journal,

The U.S. State Department, having had enough controversy about Soviet units and their capabilities for one year [i.e., the furor over the Soviet combat brigade in Cuba], refused to characterize the new force as "combat troops."[29]

That these preparations were going forward on a massive scale does not prove that the USSR had abandoned the idea of persuading Amin to sanction the intervention; they merely reflect the Soviet determination to ensure military success whether Amin concurred or not. From the standpoint of world reaction, it was still patently in Soviet interests that an invitation from Amin be secured.

On November 28, 1979, a Soviet deputy minister of internal affairs, Lieutenant General Viktor Semenovich Paputin, arrived in Kabul for official discussions on "mutual cooperation and other issues of interest."[30] The normal practice with high-level visits of this nature is to publicize them immediately; in this case there was a delay of three days before the *Kabul Times* printed the story, along with a fuzzy picture of Paputin (in dark glasses), his entourage, and the Afghan welcoming delegation. Discussions with Afghan officials (Paputin's official host was Afghan deputy minister of interior Ghulam Mustafa) reportedly began on November 30, and on December 1 he was guest of honor at a dinner hosted by the governor of Kabul province, Shah Nawaz. On the first day of the 1978 coup, Amin had appointed Mustafa as one of the two commanders of the Fifteenth Armored Division and Shah Nawaz as chief of the Commandos. The choice of Paputin's escorts thus appears not to have been fortuitous; Amin had good reason to want to have trustworthy subordinates monitoring Paputin's activities. On December 3 there was a front-page picture of Paputin being received by Amin (the latter reduced to real-life dimensions in this photo) at the People's House in Kabul.

At this point there was a hiatus in press coverage of the visit. On December 8 there was a brief note of a Politburo meeting that dealt with security affairs and an accompanying two-sentence observation that Paputin had met with Minister of Interior Faqir Mohammed Faqir. The next mention of Paputin was on the sixteenth, when the paper reported his departure three days before, "after holding friendly talks with the sources concerned" (not further elaborated). The photo that accompanied the story again portrayed a dim figure in dark glasses surrounded by large and serious Europeans, as well as some Afghans.[31]

In light of the story that was to break later, there was some question whether Paputin really departed Kabul as reported, whether he returned with the Soviet invading forces, and in either case what the nature of his final departure from Afghanistan had been. His obituary, referring to his "untimely" death on December 28, 1979 (place un-named), was published in *Pravda* and *Sovetskiy Sport* on Janu-ary 3, 1980.

Of the three stories that were to emerge on the manner of Paputin's passing, one had him killed on December 27 in yet another firefight with the redoubtable Amin, another had him mortally wounded in such an encounter,[32] and the third (probably Soviet-inspired) alleged that he had committed suicide in Moscow's Sheremetevo Airport on his return from Kabul—a result of depression at having failed in his mission. In the first two versions, Paputin's mission was allegedly to convince Amin that the latter's personal salvation, as well as that of Afghanistan, rested on his inviting Soviet troops to put down the insurgency. In the third version, his mission was to protect Amin, who was nevertheless killed "by mistake" in an accidental firefight that broke out at the Darulaman Palace.[33] However Paputin met his end, it seems to have been a violent one and directly connected with the equally violent death of Amin.

Meanwhile, from the middle of December on, Soviet intentions were emerging ever more unmistakably. Amin's nephew, Assadul-lah Amin, who was chief of the intelligence service, was seriously wounded in an assassination attempt in the presidential palace on December 17. He was evacuated for medical treatment to Tashkent, from which he returned six months later to face execution by the Babrak government for treason.[34]

On December 18 and 19 the Soviet contingent that had arrived at Bagram in mid-December was deployed along the road to the Salang Pass in order to clear the way for the 357th Mechanized Rifle Division, which was slated to come in from the north.[35] Close behind them at Bagram came a parachute regiment that landed on December 21–22.[36]

Apparently recognizing the vulnerability of the downtown Kabul presidential palace where his nephew had been wounded, Amin moved on December 22 to Darulaman Palace, a more easily defensible installation.[37] Later there were to be a number of bizarre reports on the circumstances surrounding his move to Darulaman Palace, including one report that had him going into seclusion after being voted down by his own Central Committee, which wanted to invite Soviet interven-tion. This story was doubtless nurtured by the Soviets themselves, but if it had been true, they would have been the first to identify all such

Central Committee members who had voted for intervention. In fact, those members of Amin's Central Committee who survived the invasion and the first rounds of Babrak executions soon fell into total eclipse.

The day that Amin moved to Darulaman Palace, Washington finally broke its silence on developments in Afghanistan and along the USSR's Afghan border. Previous airborne landings, plus the presence of thirty thousand Soviet troops in a high state of readiness on the Afghan border could no longer be ignored.[38]

Whether any U.S. warning, whenever tendered, would have deterred Moscow is doubtful; but in any case, by December 22 the momentum of the Soviet commitment was probably irreversible. Late on Christmas Eve the first elements of an airborne assault began landing at Kabul International Airport.

It was a well-planned, well-executed operation, one that reportedly involved several elements of sabotage and deception:

- Soviet advisors to tank forces in and around Kabul saw to it that batteries were removed from all vehicles, allegedly in order to replace them with cold-resistant, winterized ones. This removed one of the greatest hazards to the airborne operation that brought Soviet infantry directly to Kabul via the civilian airport. Just a few tanks on the runways would have frustrated this move.[39]

- The central communications complex for the government, managed by the Afghan air force, was taken over and its key officials were killed by a Soviet commando team.[40] The key figure in this operation was no less than the Soviet minister of communications himself, Nikolay Vladimirovich Talyzin. He arrived in Kabul early on December 24 for a "friendly visit," accompanied by a large retinue of burly, unsmiling aides.[41] With such a prestigious visitor on hand, the whereabouts of all key Afghan communications officials would be known to the Soviets, and the doors of otherwise closed and guarded installations would be open to the visitors.

- Arriving simultaneously with Minister Talyzin was the Uzbek republic's minister of water resources. On December 27, he and Talyzin cohosted at the Intercontinental Hotel a large reception to which leading Afghan dignitaries were invited. At the end of the festivities the guests were all arrested.[42]

Without communications, it must have been some time before Amin realized what was happening. When he did, there was no longer any opportunity for effective resistance. Throughout Christmas Day, AN-12 and AN-22 transports had been landing and taking off at Kabul airport at ever shorter intervals. From nightfall on December 25, flight density at the airport reached one in every three minutes; five thousand troops were landed by the evening of December 26.[43] Afghan officials apparently thought that the new troops were coming in as part of an authorized buildup, and there was no resistance. When Soviet troops finally went into action, their numbers and firepower were overwhelming.

H-hour was 7:15 P.M. on December 27. The Soviet troops that had been airlifted into Kabul made a coordinated attack on key government installations. Simultaneously two or three battalions, spearheaded by light tanks, struck at Darulaman Palace. Hopelessly outgunned and outnumbered, Amin and his guard nevertheless put up staunch resistance and were only overcome shortly before midnight. The wing of the palace where they made their stand was completely destroyed, and all of the defenders were wiped out. For their part, the Soviet attackers lost several vehicles and about twenty-five killed and two hundred twenty-five wounded.[44] It is probably safe to assume that Amin himself personally accounted for some of these casualties; he was a good shot.

The following day, two motorized rifle divisions crossed the frontier in three places to support the troops that had been airlifted. By January 1, 1980, fifty thousand Soviet troops were in Afghanistan and more were on the way. Four motorized infantry divisions were deployed along the Soviet-Afghan border, providing a reserve of another fifty thousand men.[45]

Amin had been a merciless Marxist dictator whose jailers and firing squads were rarely underemployed, but there was no question as to his bravery under fire. Whatever his other characteristics, his country owes him one debt of gratitude: he never tendered the Soviets the crucial invitation that would have legalized the invasion. He paid for that refusal with his life.

CHAPTER

9

Occupation Politics: The Internal Dimension
1980–1984

I am in a difficulty to know what to do with the country now we have got it.

(From an 1879 letter by General Sir Donald Stewart, after his forces occupied Kandahar during the second Anglo-Afghan War.)[1]

Such, in brief, was the country; and such were the peoples who, with no outside assistance, with no artillery but what they could capture from the enemy, with no trust but in Allah and His Prophet, their own right hands and flashing blades, defied the might of Russia for more than half a century; defeating her armies, raiding her settlements, and laughing to scorn her wealth, her pride, and her numbers.

(From an Englishman's account of the Russian conquest of the Caucasus during the eighteenth and nineteenth centuries.)[2]

From 1978 to 1980, events in Afghanistan unfolded with a certain inevitability. Those familiar with the country knew beforehand that no communist government could survive there without massive outside support, but the intensity, persistence, and pervasiveness of the resistance—spontaneous and self-supporting though it was—came as a surprise even to many Afghans. Throughout 1978 and 1979 these qualities called forth ever sharper political and military countermeasures from the Taraki and Amin governments and from the USSR. These, in turn, only stiffened the opposition. In the end, to protect its accumulated economic and political investments, the Kremlin made the ultimate military investment—an invasion and occupation.

Apparently the Soviet leaders believed that this solution, painful and filled with unknowable ramifications though it was, could not be avoided. The ultimate strategic goal of absorbing Afghanistan into the Soviet orbit ideologically, politically, economically, and militarily had not changed, but the short-term means to that end had. It would have been much more desirable in their view to have the DRA set its own house in order, aided only by such economic support and military equipment as might eventually be required to erode the resistance and prepare the country for Sovietization. Such preliminary tenderizing by the Afghans themselves would not only ease the strain of converting this basically indigestible society into something more acceptable to the Soviet organism but would also be far more tolerable in terms of international etiquette. The open military consumption of small, backward nations by larger, more modern neighbors is considered bad manners in the modern age, which continues, however, to turn a blind eye to less greedy and violent means of assimilation. Swallowing such countries whole is also, as the USSR has now discovered, remarkably difficult, but at the time the alternatives must have appeared even less appetizing.

In the short term, the USSR had several tactical goals it wished to achieve: physical disposal of the unpopular Amin and his closest followers; elimination of mujahideen (holy warrior) resistance via intimidation or, if necessary, massive military blows; and reform of the PDPA, to include removing the worst of the Amin excesses, broadening the base of popular support for the party, increasing party membership, and healing the Parcham-Khalq rift. It succeeded in the first of these objectives, the elimination of Amin, almost immediately; it has been pursuing the others doggedly but with signal lack of success ever since.

Military Factors

At the root of the Soviet difficulties, military as well as political, lies the fact that Afghanistan is less a nation than an agglomeration of some 25,000 village-states, each of which is largely self-governing and self-sufficient. There are no pan-Afghan institutions to help any central government monitor and control the countryside. Direction from the capital has traditionally been acceptable to the villagers only if it accorded generally with their own desires. Even a powerful autocrat like Abdur Rahman Khan learned to make his exemplary punishment of disobedient villages rare—if memorable—occasions. Each of his successors who inherited or seized the political reins has had to learn that running the government in Kabul does not automatically give one authority anywhere else in the country.[3]

The use of an army to enforce political decisions is complicated by the villagers' custom of fading into the hills whenever faced by the superior numbers needed to overcome their natural defenses and innate urge for self-determination. Abandonment of their meager possessions is not the sacrifice it would be in economically advanced communities, and the occupiers find little to loot. They then discover that local resources are not enough to support their presence, leaving them with the alternatives of unending resupply over vulnerable routes through hostile territory or eventual retreat. The latter is the usual choice, leaving the villagers free to return and resume their customary independent ways. Such, for example, has been the pattern in the strategic Panjshir Valley, attacked and occupied by Soviet and DRA troops no fewer than seven times in four years, yet always reverting to mujahideen control as the invaders found the costs of continued occupation intolerable.[4]

In spite of steadily increasing Soviet commitment in manpower, from 85,000 in 1979 to approximately 115,000 in 1984, the best the USSR and DRA have been able to manage so far is daytime control over the main communications links, major cities, and certain fortified strong points. The rest of the country (80–90 percent by day and virtually 100 percent after dark) is under potential or actual control by the resistance. If anything, anti-DRA forces appear to have become more assertive in the past four years, with armed attacks against Soviet and DRA targets in Kabul itself becoming more and more common. According to one secret-police defector, as of 1982 only four streets in the capital were considered safe for regime supporters or their Soviet mentors. In spring 1984, the USSR launched massive combined air-ground operations against major mujahideen targets throughout the country, its largest military offensive since the 1979 invasion—yet in its wake the major road link from the USSR was cut again and again, unti there were serious food shortages in Kabul itself. During ten days of March 1984, fifteen PDPA officials were killed by mujahideen in just one district of Kabul.[5]

So far it appears that the Soviet high command has not learned how to cope with classic guerrilla tactics, though it has been making use of a scorched-earth policy in any area from which it must retreat. From the first, the Soviets have employed terror to intimidate individual villages suspected of supporting the resistance, and this has now turned into an all-out war on civilians. Indiscriminate attacks against nonmilitary targets have become more and more common. In early 1984 a bitter history repeated itself in Istalif, just north of Kabul, a town renowned for its pottery and the scene of British atrocities against Afghan civilians during the First Anglo-Afghan War. Combined Soviet-DRA air attacks and infantry sweeps resulted in wholesale slaughter of civilians and destruction of property, setting the stage for massive attacks by Soviet forces elsewhere later in the spring.[6]

The clear intent has been to dry up the "sea" of population where, according to Mao Ze Dong, the guerrilla "fish" make their home. Villages have been razed to the ground and their inhabitants killed, driven into foreign exile, or forced into major cities where they can be more easily controlled by the authorities. Kabul alone increased in population from 700,000 in 1978 to 1.5 million in 1983. High-altitude carpet bombing by strategic aircraft was introduced in 1984, as was the use of delayed-action incendiary substances that burst into flame when stepped on. For several years toy-like miniature bombs have been regularly strewn from the air across transborder trails in order to maim the curious or the careless. The use of lethal chemical weapons ("yellow rain") appeared to have stopped as of 1984, but only after their use had led to international outrage. Major Soviet offensives have been launched against agricultural areas in order to choke off food supplies, leading to fears that up to a half-million Afghans would face starvation in 1984.[7]

This campaign has been progressive, and it is too early to assess how successful it will be in the long run. So far it has not dampened resistance enthusiasm, and the USSR can take little comfort from the nearest precedent, the nineteenth century attempt by General Yermolov to break the will of Chechen and other Muslims in the Caucasus by the use of indiscriminate terror. Though apparently effective in the short term, the long-range cost of his "system" was incalculable: after the first of his terror operations, in 1819, the Chechens unleashed a 30-year war of revenge, and, a century later, in 1944, Stalin would feel obliged to deport the entire nation to Siberia for its alleged intention to collaborate with the Germans during World War II.[8]

The immediate physical and human costs to the USSR of its Afghan adventure are already considerable. As of early 1984, the cost of the occupation was estimated at 13,500 to 30,000 Soviet casualties, $12 billion, and the destruction of 546 aircraft, 304 tanks, 436 armored personnel carriers, and 2,758 other vehicles. These figures are all subject to upward revision in the wake of the massive but abortive 1984 spring offensive.[9]

If the Soviet losses have been heavy, those of the DRA have been worse: 17,000 fatalities and 26,000 desertions have left a force of only 30,000–40,000, many of whom are collaborating with the mujahideen. The official DRA assessment of war damage suffered thus far was 24 billion afghanis in 1983 and 35 billion afghanis in 1984 (at the official rate of exchange, roughly $420,000 and $600,000). Attempting to maintain the army in the face of mass desertions, the government has resorted to the use of press-gangs to round up under- and overage conscripts. In 1982 it raised the period of compulsory service from two to three years, and in 1984 from three to four years. Exemptions were cut back at the same time, and the result, particularly in 1984, was widespread mutiny in the ranks and a further flood of desertions.[10]

The heaviest casualties among the combatants have been suffered by the mujahideen, who are estimated to have lost over 30,000. In spite of losses, however, morale has remained high through the years of Soviet occupation, and there are more and more examples of collaboration in the field between groups who in previous times would have operated independently or even at cross purposes. Prior to the 1984 Panjshir offensive, for example, coordinated attacks by various mujahideen groups on the strategic road link from Kabul to the USSR so disrupted traffic that the offensive was delayed for several weeks, and fuel for it had to be airlifted into staging areas near the capital.[11]

Internal Political Developments

The USSR's short-range political efforts in Afghanistan have met with no more success than its military thrusts. Essentially the goal was to establish the PDPA as a unified party in charge of a unified state (the DRA) that in turn would administer a pacified population. An apparent effort to separate party and state came in January 1981, when Babrak yielded his position as DRA president to Kishtmand, but the move had no visible practical consequences.

Interestingly, some of the other specific methods employed—including attempts to heal the Parcham-Khalq split, formation of the National Fatherland Front (NFF), and the use of certain non-PDPA individuals in the government—were precisely those listed in the Khalqi indictment against the alleged Parchami coup conspiracy of July/August 1978. By their actions in 1980 the DRA leaders (presumably with full Soviet support) thus implicitly confirmed the accuracy of that indictment.[12]

Soviet control of the DRA at all levels of the civil government and military establishment has been confirmed by countless defectors since the invasion. The degree of Soviet control over the PDPA is much harder to document, if only because defectors from the core of full-time party functionaries have not yet appeared. If the USSR is in fact attempting to exert such control, it is doing a remarkably poor job, for after more than four years of occupation the PDPA is still a sickly political entity, unable to rule or even to survive without Soviet military backing.

The size of the party is unknown. A review of claimed membership over time shows a rise from 18,000 at the time of the 1978 coup to roughly 40,000 in mid-1980, 63,000 in 1982, "more than 90,000" in 1983, and "more than 120,000" in 1984. All of these figures, which include both candidate (roughly half the total by official admission) and full members, are considerably inflated in most observers' opinions, with the true membership running from about a half to an eighth of the official statistics. Even taking the figures at face value, the party would constitute less than 1 percent of the population, despite repeated exhortations by PDPA leaders since the 1979 invasion to expand membership. Nevertheless, the unstinting drive to enlist new recruits has unquestionably had some effect, and since the invasion the party has continued to gain numerical strength, if irregularly.[13]

The gain in numbers, however, has been offset by a decline in quality. In 1978 Taraki declared that the party consisted mostly of schoolteachers, probably no great exaggeration in view of the intensive drive by both Parcham and Khalq in this field before 1973. By the time of a high-level party conference in 1982, however, only about half the 841 delegates had higher education, 27 were illiterate, and there were only 40 "teachers, scholars, doctors, and [members of] the creative intelligentsia."[14]

The sharp decline in the number of teachers in the PDPA is probably ascribable to the violent ill will they encountered when dispatched to rural areas as DRA and PDPA missionaries. Frequent DRA complaints about murderous resistance attacks on country schools (over 1800 are supposed to have been destroyed since 1979) provide an indication of the hazards of the profession. A Soviet author writing in 1983 claimed that 150 teachers had been slain over the preceding three years, but this is certainly a much deflated figure. The incentive for survivors to shift either their politics or their profession—or both— must be strong.[15]

Increasingly, the survival of the PDPA and DRA has depended on the military, the security police (*Sarandoy*), and the intelligence service or secret police (*Khad*). These in 1984 comprised a majority (60 percent) of the PDPA's full and candidate members—an indirect indication that only those compromised by virtue of their punitive duties on behalf of the DRA (and required by those duties to go armed) have provided a pool of willing recruits. Of the three services, the military is the most underrepresented in the party, a matter Babrak has viewed with concern, though his colleague and brother-in-law Mahmoud Baryalai claimed that "more than 60 percent" of all three security services were in the PDPA. Defecting army officers have confirmed that a relatively low percentage of military personnel join, and have alleged that many who do are merely following mujahideen instructions.[16] If all have told the approximate truth, the Sarandoy and Khad rate of membership must approach 100 percent.

Just as important as the quantity and quality of its members has been the party's inability to exercise discipline and control over the country at large and even within its own ranks. At the twelfth party plenum (July 1983) Babrak strongly criticized his subordinates for their "weak," "lazy," and "superficial" fulfillment of tenth party plenum resolutions, and for their failure to exercise adequate control over local government. In a 1984 speech to Sarandoy he told his audience that confidential files on party members' insubordination and misdeeds would make it "burn with rage." President Kishtmand in turn excoriated DRA governors for not implementing party decisions and threatened them with "investigation" for noncompliance. Summing up his own views, Babrak acknowledged that "the party is not yet our everything."[17]

As with the military situation, the inability of the central government to rule in the villages lies at the heart of the problem. If Daoud's enthusiastic young Parchami reformers discovered a "mud curtain" in the 1973 Afghan countryside, their successors have encountered far more active resistance. Daoud and the young Parchamis, for all their unpopularity, were at least accepted as Afghans; Babrak and those who support him have been viewed as quisling puppets of an alien power. A measure of their difficulties is the delay in implementing a draft law on local organs of government that was first published in September 1981, but was still under discussion at the twelfth party plenum nearly two years later.[18]

At that plenum, establishment of primary party organizations in the villages was demanded so as to give those wishing to join the PDPA ranks a place for enlistment. Even at the time, however, Babrak, in a masterpiece of understatement, acknowledged that "the sphere of activities of the party ranks and revolutionary sovereignty in some of the counties is temporarily limited."[19] A comparison of published figures shows that there were 1,656 primary party organizations in 1982, "over 2,000" in 1983, and "about 3,000" in May 1984.[20] The very vagueness of the latter figures is cause for skepticism about their accuracy, and there is no indication of how many of these organizations are actually located in the countryside rather than in secure big towns. Nevertheless, statistics do seem to indicate a growth of rural party cells: between 1983 and 1984 city and district committees apparently fell from 70 to 61 units, whereas county and sub-county committees increased from 114 to 205.[21] For its part, the DRA apparatus has tried to increase its rural authority by appointing village chiefs (*qayadars*) from Kabul, but such representatives of central power risk a rapid rate of on-site attrition. Khalqi office workers in Kabul, drafted to restore civil administration in the Panjshir valley after the summer 1982 offensive, suffered considerable losses; the survivors' bitterness was heightened by the fact that their Parchami colleagues somehow managed to evade this duty.[22]

The dimensions of the problem of overcoming village resistance are best illustrated by Babrak's call for the establishment of rural "headquarters." These were to consist of the local chiefs of all the organizations described above (Khad, Sarandoy, PDPA, the military, and the DRA), plus the NFF and its associated fronts, in order to coordinate activities and offer mutual support. Although it is too soon to assess the long-term effects of these various measures, military successes by the resistance in the countryside to date show that pacification still eludes the authorities.[23]

Another basic weakness of the PDPA has been the continued failure to heal the split between its Parchami and Khalqi wings. Except for the eleventh party plenum, devoted entirely to economic affairs, all plenums from the invasion through March 1984 have contained loud but ineffective demands for unity. The split, although usually treated delicately by the authorities ("the tingling noise of struggle" was one official euphemism), remains as serious as ever and occasionally provokes more revealing phraseology: "Fist and sword do not have a place in the party," Babrak told a Sarandoy audience in April 1984. "The equipment and military means given to you are not to be used in the party." Criticizing the rampant indiscipline in the party, he outlined the main PDPA task in 1984 as the "struggle against manifestations and inclinations of fractionism, sectar[ian]ism, chauvinism, local and expansionist nationalism, left-wing tendency [sic] and adventurism, dogmatism, all types of right and left-wing opportunism and liberalism."[24] (He was not merely indulging in hyperbole: in August 1983 Parchami army officers and Khalqi policemen engaged in a firefight near Herat that left about one hundred killed and wounded on both sides.)[25]

Fortunately for the mujahideen, the Parcham-Khalq split is most vigorously represented in the three security services. If the military, Khad, and Sarandoy could cooperate fully they would pose a much greater threat to the resistance. Khad is estimated to have about 20,000 members, Sarandoy about the same, and the Afghan army 30,000–40,000. But Sarandoy, under its brusque leader, General Gulabzoy, is dominated by Khalqis, whereas Khad is a stronghold of Parchamis. The military is less polarized as a whole, but individual units tend to follow the politics of their Parchami or Khalqi commanders, and the result has been at best obstruction among the services and at worst armed conflict.

Attempts to bridge the gap between the people and the PDPA/DRA by promoting front groups have shown little sign of success. Since 1978, institutions patterned after Soviet labor unions, youth and women's groups, unions of writers and artists, peasants' associations, and similar organizations have been set up or taken over by the PDPA, but have not enjoyed popularity. An overall umbrella organization to coordinate these groups was proposed on several occasions after the

1978 coup but only came into being with the founding of the National Fatherland Front in June 1981.[26]

As with the party, the size of the NFF is open to question. The official claim in mid-1983 was 600,000 members in 410 committees. A later news release may inadvertently have given the correct membership when it claimed 55,000 members in "more than 1,000 committees."[27]

Despite its intent to bridge the gap between the people and their government, the NFF has no popular appeal and has been largely unable to fulfill directives on increasing its rural membership. Within a month after its official founding, twenty-seven NFF members had been asassinated by the mujahideen, including a ranking noncommunist on the Executive Committee, retired general Fateh Mohammed.[28]

Reminiscent of an abortive attempt by Amin to set up Committees for Defense of the Revolution has been a whole complex of civilian militias, operating under such names as soldiers of the revolution, revolution defense groups, civil defense, regional battalions, and self-defense groups. These formations appear to consist of volunteers employed at a given site, whose duty it is to defend DRA property against attacks by the mujahideen. The implication is that their weapons are secured at the work place. This might help to prevent arms from falling into mujahideen hands, but it leaves the volunteers in a most vulnerable condition during their off-duty time. Claimed membership for these volunteers is 23,000, of which 9,000 are members of agricultural cooperatives.[29]

Propaganda and Longer Term Politico-Economic Programs

Although much of the foregoing analysis is based on official publications, the overall picture of domestic developments painted by the Afghan media is, of course, roseate. In spite of the DRA/PDPA's disrepute in the eyes of the overwhelming majority of Afghans, they have been able to project at least the image of authority and prestige they so badly need. With tireless and tiresome consistency, the media have reiterated themes supporting the government, the party, and the front groups, in the obvious hope that repetition will eventually beget belief. Several new publications have made their appearance in order to spread the government's message, and in mid-1983 an East German team installed new equipment at Radio Kabul enabling the station to increase its broadcasts from twenty-nine hours a week to forty. By 1984 the *Kabul New Times* was appearing in a bold new format with larger headlines, if still in only four pages.[30]

Among the most common themes are those designed to convince the reader that the regime is secure. The proclaimed release of prisoners from jail is a theme that did not die with Amin but has been repeated with unfailing regularity. Another is the series devoted to the return of happy Afghans from Pakistani refugee camps. Under the oft-encountered headline "Deceived return," the articles are supposed to undo the negative image provided by some 3 million refugees living just beyond the Afghan borders in Iran and Pakistan. Similarly, under such leaders as "Miscreants annihilated" one finds stories of resistance groups having been cut to pieces by DRA (never by Soviet) troops or militia. Starting in 1983 such stories took on a more triumphant tone, often alleging that the backbone of the resistance had been broken, a claim belied by that same resistance's enduring and vigorous offensive actions.

One of the most assiduously pursued and least successful propaganda campaigns has been the effort to portray Babrak as a religious believer and the DRA as an Islamic state. Whatever credibility this campaign might have achieved was so eroded by mid-1983 that the regime was pressed into using the same renegade Muslim cleric, Sayed Bahawoddin Jan Aqa, over and over again. In a series of news articles that spanned several weeks, in each of which his name was spelled differently in order to make him seem a different person, Aqa's meetings with various DRA/PDPA leaders were described in detail.[31]

Another method of boosting government supporters' flagging morale has been the granting of medals and promotions. In September 1982, six colonels were promoted to general, and the following April the regime announced it had bestowed over 4,700 orders and medals and made over 11,000 "extraordinary" promotions in the armed forces since January 1, 1980. Indiscriminate promotion of officers resulted in one Gilbert and Sullivan situation where a DRA unit had 20 brigadiers for 400 troops.[32]

Parallel to media campaigns harshly critical of the West in general and supporting all things Soviet has been the formation of various groups to promote Soviet acculturation. Friendship societies with all pro-Soviet countries have been founded, and there has been a busy exchange program of visits between related front groups. In the case of the Soviet-Afghan Friendship Society, during June 1983 there was a spate of news articles describing the opening of Soviet "friendship chambers" in dozens of Afghan ministries and enterprises.[33] These have resulted in no marked rise in Soviet popularity.

Longer range programs to establish Soviet control have also been set in motion, among them the whole field of education. Ever since the 1978 coup there has been a widely trumpeted effort to increase literacy in the country, and the texts used in this program are written and printed in the USSR. Special Russian-language courses lasting one year were introduced after the invasion and, as of June 1983, this project had graduated 800 students. By the end of 1983 the DRA was claiming a million students in primary schools and 200,000 in 469 secondary schools. In mid-1983 the authorities reported a Kabul University student body of 6,700 in three fields (faculties), of whom 2,400 were women and 3,000 came from rural areas. There were 900 government officials taking night courses, and the faculty consisted of 40 Afghan and 60 foreign lecturers and instructors from "friendly countries." At the start of the next year's term there were 1,030 women and 793 men newly enrolled in the university.[34]

These statistics are disputed by defectors, who place the Kabul University student body at a maximum of 5,000, most of whom are women. Up to 80 percent of the university faculty had fled as of 1983; in the faculty of law, only 4 out of 30 Afghan teachers remained. Even if regime statistics were correct, the enrollment would be less than half the 14,000 students registered in 1973. The figures for primary and secondary schools seem unlikely in view of resistance control of the countryside.[35]

In any case, as of 1984 it appears that university enrollment will sink both quantitatively and qualitatively. Previously, vocational school and university students were exempt from military duty as long as they could maintain passing grades. Only if they had to repeat a year twice did they become vulnerable to conscription. Meantime, however, new regulations permitted demobilized soldiers to enter higher educational institutions without taking the entrance examinations demanded of those who had not served. This led to a boycott by outraged civilian students at Kabul University in October 1983. Worse, however, was to come: in March 1984 the new regulations that demanded four years of military service for each draftee also dictated that no student who had not fulfilled his military duty obligation would be admitted to a university or considered for study abroad. Those already studying would continue to be deferred—but were vulnerable for instant conscription if they suffered but one academic failure.[36]

The demand that military service precede any study abroad will, if strictly enforced, severely limit what is often perceived in the West as the most insidious and threatening long-range Soviet program: educating Afghans inside the USSR and Eastern Europe. The concern is that these young people, separated from their culture for long periods, indoctrinated with communist propaganda, speaking fluent Russian, and very often recruited by one of the bloc intelligence services, will return to administer the country according to Soviet wishes. The estimated 4,000 students in bloc countries at the end of 1979 was supposed to have risen to 7,000 in 1981. Estimates since then have ranged up to 25,000 in the USSR alone. According to consistent reporting from the *Kabul New Times*, however, agreements on educating Afghan civilians in the USSR have envisaged sending a steady 1,500 per year through 1988. Far fewer study in other bloc countries, and the total number of Afghans studying abroad at any given time is unlikely to be over 6,000.[37]

Those analysts who pluck most noisily at their worry beads point to the success enjoyed by the USSR in recruiting Afghan military officers in the pre-1978 era. They predict a similar level of success against today's civilian students, who, they imply, will return with modern skills and Soviet convictions to take over from the current crop of discredited leaders. Moreover, an Institute of Social Sciences, established in Kabul after the invasion, is supposed to have trained 2,500 party members by mid-1982, providing a cadre of ideologues to work alongside the Soviet-trained technocrats.[38]

In the very long run such pessimism may be justified, but not for many years. Afghan students in the USSR have encountered racial prejudice and hostility because of Soviet casualties in their country. Some students have clashed with police. Even if some obtain valuable training and avoid conflict, no educational program can carry as much psychological weight as the reality they return to: a native land under alien military occupation, where their compatriots heroically resist that occupation, and the small ruling clique suffers under a pall of popular contempt. Little wonder that, after more than six years of communist rule and perhaps as many as 10,000 returned graduates, there is only a continuing decay in the economy, heightened insecurity in town and countryside, growing despair of the DRA's political administration, and no easing of hatred for the Soviet occupiers. Whatever the ultimate benefits to the USSR, the educational program has not worked yet.

Another long-range program is an offshoot of the education drive. Under the enticing slogan "national and cultural rights to be ensured," each minority nationality in the Afghan community of peoples is being promised its own language and literature. The eventual goal is to reduce grass-roots communication and hence cooperation among the various tribes, with Russian in the end becoming the only common language. Moscow used the same technique as part of its colonization of Central Asia, where the strategy helped to dissipate opposition. With a population that is only slightly literate and unlikely to submit to government schooling while the resistance holds sway, Afghanistan will not be so easy a target for such a divide-and-rule strategy. Nevertheless, newspapers and radio broadcasts in some minority languages have already been established, and more will doubtless follow.[39]

The establishment of Soviet-style economic institutions has been another long-range program designed to promote centralized control. The best-known such Soviet instrument is the collective farm, Stalin's tool for subduing rebellious peasants. In Afghanistan the regime is careful to avoid the term collective, but the "productive cooperatives" are designed to fulfill the same role. These cooperatives were established in conjunction with a land reform program that has gone through convulsions in response to political changes in the country. Immediately after the 1978 coup some 300,000 poor and landless peasant families allegedly were given property confiscated from the rich, and 1,300 cooperatives were established. A debacle ensued, because no provision for water rights, agricultural loans, or machinery use had been made. The old institutions had been pulled down, but there were no new ones to take their place. When Babrak took power, in a vain bid to gain popularity he actually reversed land reform and promised cooperative tribal leaders unlimited acreage for their personal use. Inasmuch as these leaders were already administering their territories independent of any DRA wishes, the gesture netted him little.[40]

In 1982 land reform got under way again, but at a far slower rate. As of 1983, 350,000 peasant families had received deeds since 1978, but only 9,200 of these had been meted out since the invasion (of which

6,000 had benefited in the year ending March 1983). Meanwhile, the number of cooperatives had shrunk to less than 100, though plans were laid for 25 new ones to be established in 1983–84.[41]

Since 1978 agricultural production has declined drastically. The DRA has put the best face on the decline by describing yields in terms of the local currency (afghanis), a method that permits the authorities to claim modest percentage gains (e.g., from 82.1 billion afghanis in 1978–79 to 86.6 billion afghanis in 1982–83.) This system conveniently ignores a galloping inflation that has seen a fourfold increase in retail prices of all basic commodities since 1979. Real production according to the official statistics is thus about a quarter of what it was in the first post-coup year. That approximation is close to the 1983 crop estimate made by an Afghan agricultural expert who defected from the DRA and who placed the figure at about one-fifth or one-quarter of the 1978 harvest. Massive imports of grain and other edibles from the Soviet Union in 1982, 1983, and 1984 confirm that Afghan agriculture can no longer support even the diminished population that remains after the refugee exodus. Another sign was the distribution of 250,000 food ration coupons to workers in 1983, permitting the purchase of 28 kilograms of flour per month for single people, 56 kilograms for families.[42]

The DRA figures on gross national product (GNP) and national income must also be assessed in the light of inflation. The supposed increase of 6 percent in GNP and 4.5 percent in national income between 1983 and 1984 was based on figures of 168.4 billion afghanis and 118.7 billion afghanis, respectively. The currency, however, had devalued drastically in the interim. The fact that state expenditures in 1983 were supposed to total 3.2 billion afghanis while planned revenues were only 340 million afghanis is a clear portent of more inflation to come. In 1984, new publicity was given to the "import and distribution" firm Kart, a government retail sales organization apparently designed to squeeze the individual Afghan merchant out of business. Kart's long-range purpose, like that of the agricultural cooperatives, is probably to eliminate private enterprise. Because its natural habitat is urban, not rural, it stands a somewhat better chance of success than the cooperatives, which must fight for survival in an environment dominated by the resistance.[43]

The Catch-22 situation in which the DRA finds itself is that the tested Soviet techniques for establishing complete control all require a degree of control to start with. So far the fighting mujahideen have denied the DRA that minimal foothold. Instead, it is now the mujahideen themselves who are stepping outside their traditional role as purely fighting men and setting up political structures. Granted, there is no single dominating ideology (the orientation of mujahideen leaders ranges from the most orthodox religious to the most modern secular), nor is there yet a single government-in-exile or a single resistance command inside the country. Nevertheless, leaders like the Panjshir Valley's Ahmad Shah Massoud have responded to the local survival needs of the population by setting up practical political and economic institutions in parallel with their military structures. The Panjshir is divided into districts (*qaragah*) and subdistricts, each of which is ruled over by committees for military, economic, political, judicial, and social affairs. Local schools with both religious and secular teachers have been established, taxes are levied, and in one province there is even supposed to be a mujahideen postal system with its own stamps. A network of clandestine FM radio transmitters broadcasts resistance news and commentary throughout the country, beaming their message not only to Afghan audiences but to Soviet troops as well. One of the remarkable features of the Panjshir system is that it has spread beyond the confines of its native valley into surrounding areas, possibly constituting the nucleus for a post-Soviet Afghan government in the distant future.[44]

In the end, the question boils down to one of survival. If the Afghan resistance can keep a subsistence economy functioning in liberated areas in spite of Soviet military sweeps, there is no way that the USSR can win its war. If, on the other hand, the USSR succeeds in its stepped-up military actions, in the end rural Afghanistan will be reduced to a wasteland incapable of supporting a viable resistance.

CHAPTER

10

Occupation Politics: The External Dimension
1980–1984

There is no necessity to insist on the palpable interest of Russia in restricting the growth of her territory and preventing the advent of complications in distant provinces which may retard and paralyze our domestic development.

(From a memorandum by Prince Gorchakov dated November 21, 1864, in relation to Russian expansion in Central Asia)[1]

Imposing unpopular regimes on unwilling people by military force is a Soviet tradition. By the end of World War II this practice had not only established the present borders of the USSR but extended a modified Soviet control over the nominally independent countries of Eastern Europe. Thereafter, Soviet forces honored the custom by stamping out periodic efforts by these peoples to reassert their independence: the Germans in 1953, Hungarians in 1956, and Czechs (the only Warsaw Pact country where communism had not been installed by Soviet occupation forces) in 1968. These repressions have been neither comfortable nor cheap for successive Kremlin leaders, but the strategic value of western footholds apparently outweighed the considerable political and economic cost of retaining them. The sudden, massive, military blow, whatever its long-term costs in national hatreds, had proven an effective method for preserving Moscow's hegemony.

In Afghanistan the Soviet military commitment, though no less massive and sudden than those seen in Europe, has had a completely different outcome. The European operations were successful first because they took place on territory that had been tacitly ceded by the

USSR's World War II allies as an area of Soviet domination; second, because they had been launched against small, relatively modern European powers with which the vast majority of the world could not identify; and, third—perhaps most important—because they were successful in crushing all physical resistance in a matter of days if not hours.

In Afghanistan, none of these conditions has applied.

Although the country traditionally had maintained a foreign policy that was far more obliging to Moscow's than to Washington's interests, and though the 1978 communist coup had been unopposed in the West, Afghanistan was never acknowledged to be under Soviet dominion. The Kremlin leaders were fully aware that military occupation of this territory would seriously jolt their relations with the rest of the world. With direct control over a sixth of the earth's land surface and political authority over a good deal more, Soviet leaders could logically predict that there would be some resentment against yet another extension of their empire. They were correct. To invade, Leonid Brezhnev later acknowledged, was "no simple decision."[2]

International Reactions to the Invasion

Brezhnev unquestionably underestimated, however, the extent and depth of the reaction, especially by the USSR's chief rival, the United States. In the period before the invasion, the United States had gained an international reputation for uncertainty and vacillation in its foreign policy. This, coupled with the USSR's own growing confidence in its improving military capabilities and its perception of a shifting "correlation of forces" in its favor, must have made it feel that it could weather whatever improvised response to the invasion President Carter might devise.[3] Indeed, among the options that Washington chose to pursue most were predictable, yet the cumulative impact was perhaps more than the USSR had bargained for.

Moscow almost certainly reckoned with the loss of SALT II, the strategic arms limitation agreement that had been hammered out after many years of negotiation. In early 1980 this seemed doomed to die for want of support in the U.S. Senate anyway, and all that was at risk was the loss of presidential lobbying on behalf of the measure. Similarly, the suspension of negotiations for a new agreement on scientific and cultural exchanges was a predictable penalty, but one that the USSR probably expected (mistakenly) would be as short-lived as similar steps taken in the wake of the 1968 invasion of Czechoslovakia.

The most significant U.S. economic sanction was the suspension of wheat exports to the USSR. Though a relatively easy way for America to show its displeasure, such a move in an election year may have been considered by Soviet analysts to be beyond the political courage of President Carter. Even pessimists among them could point (in this case justifiably) to the likelihood that domestic economic and political considerations would force resumption of the shipments before very long. Such views were vindicated when President Reagan lifted the embargo on April 24, 1981, less than sixteen months after its imposition.[4]

More worrisome to the USSR must have been the prospect that its action would accelerate rapprochement between the United States and China. Moscow, however, could assume that even such a dramatic event as the invasion would not have much effect one way or the other on the improvement in Sino-American relations, a glacially slow but seemingly irresistible process that the USSR could see little way of deterring in any case.

Finally, the U.S. boycott of the 1980 Moscow summer Olympic games was a step that almost certainly came as a rude surprise to the USSR, and it was one that rankled more deeply than most Americans realized. The Soviet craving for recognition and respect in the international community is extraordinarily keen, and the boycott was taken as a direct assault on the USSR's prestige. Again, there must have been an assumption that domestic U.S. politics would rule out any such step in an election year. When the United States was joined in the boycott by many allied and neutral states, the USSR was clearly discomfited.[5]

More fundamentally, however, the invasion marked a watershed in U.S.-Soviet relations. These had already become strained after Soviet deployment of SS-20 missiles targeted on Western Europe had upset the NATO–Warsaw Pact balance of forces. The two-track negotiating posture of the United States—commitment to arms limitation via negotiations if possible, and commitment to NATO deployment of Pershing II and cruise missiles if negotiations failed—was designed to safeguard the achievements of détente as long as possible without sacrificing adequate deterrence. The hope that the USSR could be talked out of its SS-20s was, however, almost certainly a vain one; it became merely an academic question when the Afghan invasion set in motion a groundswell of anti-Soviet public opinion in the United States. In practical terms, that groundswell in 1980 provided wide public support for an expanded defense budget while the Carter administration was still in office—and then saw that administration swept away by a lopsided majority in the next election. The accelerated Soviet arms programs made some such development inevitable, but the invasion of Afghanistan provided the critical catalyst for the American response.

America's NATO allies were less firm in their immediate reactions against the USSR, though most joined in the Olympics boycott. With a recession looming, they were wary of jeopardizing lucrative contracts with the USSR and made no move comparable to the U.S. economic sanctions, thus rousing some bitterness in American circles. Here the optimists among Soviet foreign policy experts would have been correct: European short-term economic interests clearly overrode any incentive to take an unyielding stand on principle.

If the reaction of the United States and its allies was more or less predictable, that of the Third World probably was not. Over the years the USSR had become accustomed to Third World approval, or at least benign disregard, of almost any action it chose to take, even military actions against neighboring states. The events of 1953, 1956, and 1968 in Eastern Europe had provoked only the mildest of rebukes outside Europe and North America, and there might have been some Soviet illusion that their Afghan adventure would produce an equally bland reaction.

But if Third World nations had seen no reason to object to one set of rich Caucasians beating on another, they were strenuously opposed to rich Caucasians beating on poor non-Caucasians. Moreover, Afghanistan was a country with which most could identify: economically backward, politically unstable, militarily weak, and historically under great power pressure or occupation. The initial UN General Assembly vote on a resolution that all foreign troops be withdrawn from the country was the worst defeat suffered by the USSR in that forum since the Korean War; subsequent votes have shown no flagging in Third World support for the measure (see Table 1). Even more than the size of the vote, its consistency over so long a period constitutes a debilitating drain on Soviet prestige.

TABLE 1
UN GENERAL ASSEMBLY VOTING PATTERNS
ON WITHDRAWAL OF FOREIGN TROOPS FROM AFGHANISTAN

Date	Votes for	Votes against	Abstentions
January 1980	104	18	18
November 1980	111	22	12
November 1981	116	23	12
November 1982	114	21	13
November 1983	116	20	17

Votes in other international forums since the invasion have confirmed these sentiments. The DRA was suspended from the Islamic Conference at an emergency meeting in Islamabad in January 1980, and in May the regular meeting of that group called for the "immediate, unconditional, and total withdrawal" of Soviet troops.[6] In Geneva the United Nations Human Rights Commission has consistently voted for withdrawal of foreign forces from the country. Even the Conference of Non-Aligned Nations, normally most solicitous of Soviet sensitivities, at its 1983 New Delhi meeting voted over the strenuous objections of pro-Soviet members for a "political settlement" on the basis of "the withdrawal of foreign troops."[7] None of this has motivated the USSR to reverse its policies, but the political price it is paying for the occupation will continue to mount as long as the resistance holds out.

The Pakistan Sanctuary

At first the USSR responded to its image problem in typically Soviet fashion: it tried to make Afghanistan un-news. Western correspondents were banned from the country in January and February 1980, and Soviet media simply ignored the war. Under similar circumstances in Europe, the USSR had succeeded in imposing a news blackout by sealing the borders of its rebellious states. Afghanistan's border, which runs through extremely rugged territory inhabited by tribes resistant to central control even in the best of circumstances, could not be sealed. Across the border has poured the greatest refugee migration of the modern age, eventually to settle in Pakistan (over 2 million) and

Iran (1–1.5 million).[8] Each refugee is a source of information on what is happening in the country; the news blackout has not succeeded.

Back across the border have gone the bands of mujahideen fighters who, having left their dependents behind in the refugee camps, are free to fight the invaders unencumbered. (Occasionally they are accompanied by intrepid journalists and cameramen, whose coverage of events inside also keeps the Afghanistan story alive in the world's press.) Crossing again with their wounded, the mujahideen find a safe haven and medical assistance—and a quagmire of emigré politicking that must be almost as discouraging as any military action against them by DRA or Soviet opponents in their homeland.

No fewer than seven major resistance groups have formed, all competing for foreign financial, humanitarian, and military aid. Much of this comes from rich Islamic oil-producing nations of the region, but there has been no known effort to coordinate the aid in a manner that would make it more effective. The seven emigré groups are divided into two general groupings, the fundamentalists and the moderates, and, despite periodic gestures toward union, they have invariably fallen victim to traditional Afghan fractiousness. Those doing the actual fighting are disgusted with this turn of events, but because it is the Pakistan-based emigrés who have the foreign contacts who in turn provide the needed supplies, the fighters must accommodate themselves to the petty intrigues of the various self-styled leaders. The developing cooperation in the field among the mujahideen stands in refreshing contrast to the bickering of the noncombatant exile politicians, who by their conceit and ambition often serve Soviet purposes almost as well as Babrak Karmal himself.

The USSR has been an active participant in these intrigues. Having gotten its own start as a minor emigré movement in Europe, and having done battle ever since with its own exiles, the CPSU is keenly aware of the capabilities and vulnerabilities of emigré movements. Soviet techniques of assault on emigré targets range from the brutal and direct to the extremely subtle and sophisticated. At one end of the spectrum are the assassins who try to eliminate the most effective leaders. At the other are infiltrators tasked not with disrupting the activities of a group but with monitoring and eventually controlling them. A method that has been in vogue since tsarist days involves artificially promoting an agent within a group by actively furthering his career. Often this can be a "security expert," to whom other Soviet penetration agents (unaware of their role as sacrificial lambs) can be fed and then "unmasked," allowing the agent to work his way up to a position of absolute trust and full knowledgeability.

In early 1983 one Western correspondent estimated that 80 percent of the Soviet effort against the mujahideen was devoted to subversion and only 20 percent to conventional counterinsurgency operations.[9] If true, the results from all this effort were not impressive within Afghanistan, a conclusion the Soviet high command may also have reached: the heightened military activity of 1983 and 1984 indicates that direct assault had again come into fashion. As noted in the previous chapter, the closeknit Afghan village society is next to impossible to subvert. The exile community abroad, however, consists largely of persons unknown to each other and is extremely vulnerable to such activity.

Foreign Military and Humanitarian Aid

For all their intriguing, however, the emigré leaders have kept the channels of foreign aid open to those doing the fighting. Contrary to DRA and Soviet charges, there was no American involvement in supplying arms to the mujahideen before the invasion, but immediately thereafter President Carter authorized a program of covert military assistance. That program continued and eventually expanded under President Reagan. Soviet weaponry stored or produced in Egypt was purchased there in limited quantities, some of it by Saudi Arabia, and then transported via Pakistan to the resistance. (Pakistan, concerned with its vulnerability to Soviet pressure, allegedly placed three conditions on such aid crossing its territory: no public acknowledgment by any of the participants in the arms lift; immediate movement of all supplies out of Pakistan and into Afghanistan; and a limit of about two planeloads per week.)[10] By 1983 the operation was alleged to be costing $30 to $50 million per year, of which the United States was paying about half. A year later American aid was estimated to have risen to $80 million.[11] These are relatively minuscule amounts compared to the estimated $4 billion the occupation is now costing Moscow each year, and in the opinion of many it is an inadequate level of support.

Although other NATO countries apparently have not taken part in the arms lift, there have been contributions by European individuals and volunteer organizations that have earned well-deserved respect both in Afghanistan and abroad. Most prominent among these are three French volunteer medical groups—Aide Médicale Internationale, Médicins sans Frontières, and Médicins du Monde—that regularly have sent unpaid doctors and nurses on hazardous missions into the country to treat mujahideen and civilian sufferers alike.[12] In addition to their humanitarian mission, these volunteers have returned with accounts of life inside Afghanistan that have helped to keep the issue of Soviet brutality against Afghan civilians alive and thus perhaps to deter Soviet forces from even worse excesses.

Soviet International Tactics

Having failed to present the world with a fait accompli—a destroyed resistance and an established DRA controlled by the PDPA—the USSR settled down patiently to erode and subvert the opposition to its invasion that had sprung up outside Afghanistan while stepping up its terrorist tactics inside. Its broad strategy has been to wear down external opposition by simply outwaiting it, exploiting the fickleness of world public interest in a little-known land and the eagerness of those who do care about the country to halt the bloodshed. The USSR's stated position from the outset has been that its "limited contingent" of troops will remain until the "external threat" (i.e., the resistance) has been removed. With various modifications it has insisted, in effect, on international guarantees for the Babrak Karmal regime (or one equally amenable to Soviet direction) as the price for its withdrawal. The Soviets have demonstratively welcomed efforts by UN Undersecretary Diego Cordovez to mediate among Pakistan, Iran, Afghanistan, and the USSR in order to reach a peaceable solution, but in spite of periodic optimistic progress reports, no resolution of the conflict appears likely as the sixth year of occupation approaches.[13]

In addition to patience, Moscow has made use of three overlapping techniques to sap foreign support for the resistance: establishing a monopoly over Afghanistan's foreign trade; applying direct and indirect political pressure on non-Soviet-bloc countries; and unleashing a broad campaign of disinformation.

Economic Exploitation

Soviet economic exploitation of Afghanistan follows a classic colonial pattern, with some twentieth century modifications. Although rich in untapped natural resources such as copper and iron ore, Afghanistan has only one source of mineral wealth now being exploited: natural gas. In the 1950s Moscow successfully pressured the royal Afghan government to prevent West European or American oil and gas exploration in the northern provinces. Later, the USSR conducted such exploration itself and, after finding a rich pocket of gas at Shebergan, began extracting it.

As of 1983, an estimated 95 percent of the gas produced there flowed directly into the Soviet Central Asian pipeline network, with the remaining 5 percent (300 million cubic meters, according to Afghan figures) withheld as the primary ingredient for the Shebergan fertilizer plant. This would indicate a total annual production of 6.0 billion cubic meters, though the Afghans claim only 2.7 billion were produced in 1982, of which the USSR received 2.4 billion. Earlier plans to raise production to 3.0 billion cubic meters appear to have been shelved, and both the volume received and the credits given by the USSR for the gas were to remain the same in 1984 as 1983. The price allegedly paid for the gas is about $12 per thousand cubic meters, less than what the Soviets charge Western Europe for their own natural gas but "several times over" what they paid Afghanistan for the same product before the PDPA came to power.[14]

The Soviet generosity, however, bears closer examination. First, the Afghans today receive no money for the gas; they only receive credit on a debt to the USSR that is estimated conservatively at $3 billion. Unlike such other recipients of Soviet aid as Cuba and Vietnam, the Afghans receive no military hardware free of charge; they also must pay an undisclosed amount of the Soviet occupation costs. With no chance of ever being paid in full for their equipment and presence, the Soviets get the benefit of appearing generous by raising the purchase price of the natural gas. The only benefit to the Afghans is a debt that is smaller on paper but still immeasurably beyond the country's means to pay.[15] Second, when the pipeline into Central Asia was completed in 1968, Soviet engineers thoughtfully placed the meter on the Soviet side of the border; no one on the Afghan side has ever known how much gas actually passes through the line.[16]

Aside from natural gas, Afghan exports to the USSR in 1984 were to include dried and fresh fruit, pelts, wool, and cotton. In return the Afghans were to receive sugar, wheat, vegetable oil, petroleum products, matches, dried milk, textiles, medicines, machinery, vehicles, tires, liquid gas, and chemical fertilizer, with a total trade volume of $911 million, 8 percent above the comparable figure in 1983. In addition, the USSR obligated itself to provide the DRA with a grant-in-aid of $112 million in 1984, the aid items to include wheat, sugar, fuel, textiles, vehicles, and household goods. The DRA confessed that exports during the first half of 1983, while "satisfactory," had not matched the $184 million of imports from the USSR.[17]

Between 1978 and 1983 commercial intercourse with nations belonging to the Council on Mutual Economic Assistance (Comecon) rose from 40 percent to 70 percent of all Afghan trade. Compared with the period 1976–1980, trade with the USSR from 1981 to 1985 was to treble. Afghanistan was also one of the four countries that collectively received 86 percent of all Soviet foreign aid (estimated at $8 billion in 1983). A substantial portion of the aid is in the form of essential commodities, including food and textiles.[18]

The Soviet colonial approach is also shown in Afghanistan's investment pattern. Although 70 percent of the country's population is employed in agriculture, and although the war's destruction has been fiercest in farming areas, economic planning for 1982–83 called for 37.6 percent of investment to be in mines and industry, 27.4 percent in transportation, and only 10.4 percent in agriculture.[19]

Perhaps the most ominous economic note was an innocuous-looking item in the Afghan press in late 1983 reporting that "border trade" between Afghanistan and the Soviet Central Asian republics of Tajikistan, Uzbekistan, and Turkmenistan had amounted to over $1.2 million in a recent six-month period (probably March to September 1983), a 250 percent rise over the same period the previous year.[20] The implication is that the trade is being handled as if it were an internal Soviet matter instead of an international exchange, implying that Afghanistan was on the road to economic, if not political, integration into the USSR.

All of these measures are designed to isolate Afghanistan from the West and to cut off any noncommunist economic interest in securing the country's freedom.

Political Pressure and Disinformation

As noted previously, the USSR has continued to receive regular reprimands from the United Nations and other international forums for its invasion and occupation. It is noteworthy, however, that almost none of the resolutions refer to the USSR by name. Instead, although everyone is aware of the culprit's identity, the demand is usually couched in an impersonal call for the removal of "all foreign troops." The circumlocution is not accidental. At the Non-Aligned Nations Conference in Cuba in 1982, for example, Pakistan tried to introduce a resolution specifically condemning the USSR for its invasion, but was voted down. Nor is it merely an exhibition of international good manners: in resolutions where the United States has been censured, such as those regarding the Grenada operation, no bones were made about assigning blame to the United States, even though other nations were also involved.[21]

Directly or indirectly, it can also be assumed that Moscow has put pressure on Pakistan to prevent arms aid to the mujahideen from reaching unacceptably high levels. Among the potential threats the Soviets could voice might be political destabilization of General Zia's somewhat shaky dictatorship or hot pursuit of mujahideen into Pakistani territory. The Soviet invasion of Afghanistan, however, has probably helped consolidate Zia's rule, as Pakistanis realized they had to pull together to counter the threat from the north. Regarding hot pursuit, the unforeseeable consequences of such action, given U.S. implicit guarantees to Pakistan, would make any such move too risky; the threat would be recognized as a bluff. Nevertheless, Pakistan's exposed position makes it understandably nervous, a condition the USSR is unlikely to have overlooked.

The spread of disinformation—the deliberate creation of false images ascribed to non-Soviet sources in order to promote Soviet interests—appears to stand a better chance of producing results than political arm twisting. The technique is one that the USSR has developed to a high degree over many years, having established a special department within the KGB for such operations in 1959.[22] Disinformation can take many forms, including forged documents designed to discredit their supposed originator or his country. These usually are fairly easy to expose, but only after they have created an impression that can linger on even after their origin is proven false.

The use of a witting or unwitting agent with noncommunist credentials (often called an "agent of influence") to propagate a desired false theme is a more subtle technique. It involves a delicate balance between projecting a false theme that serves Soviet interests while preserving the bona fides of the author as a knowledgeable person uncommitted to the communist cause. When successful, this method can be both effective and hard to expose as a Soviet operation. (Is the writer who makes a demonstrably wrong analysis that coincidentally fits Soviet needs working wittingly for the KGB? Is he the unwitting victim of others sent to mislead him? Or does he just have bad judgment? It is easy to become hypersensitive and to see the KGB hand where it does not exist, yet Soviet covert manipulation of media is too well documented to brush off as imagination.)[23]

In Afghanistan what looks suspiciously like a preplanned Soviet disinformation campaign got under way during and immediately after the 1978 coup. While the outcome of the coup was still in doubt, no mention was made of the PDPA or its role in Daoud's overthrow. So small was the party that its chances for success, had the Afghan people realized what was happening, were minimal. Until Daoud and the other ranking Mohammedzai family members were safely dead or under arrest, and until leftist officers could cement their control over most of the country's military units, it would have been potentially fatal to acknowledge that a communist coup had occurred. Thus, it was General Abdul Qader who, as head of a "Military Revolutionary Council," ostensibly ran the country in the first critical days before the outcome was assured. Only after that did Taraki and the PDPA take over, but even then attempts to disguise the Marxist-Leninist nature of the new regime continued in the Afghan and foreign press for some time.[24]

In more recent times, news coverage beneficial to Soviet interests has pursued several different lines. One is that U.S. policy on Afghanistan, through stupidity or evil conniving, is at best counterproductive and at worst malign. Quite obviously, U.S. policy on Afghanistan or any other issue is far from perfect and is deserving of the intelligent criticism it regularly receives. Some specific critiques, however, deserve examination. For example, when the question of resuming grain shipments to the USSR was being debated in 1981, an effort was made to tip the scales by suggesting that the embargo had been a mistake because it had spurred the Soviets to "reform and modernize" agriculture, thus strengthening the Soviet system.[25] Conveniently overlooked was the fact that the insoluble Soviet crisis in agriculture has endured ever since collectivization—and that in any case nothing could suit U.S. purposes better than a Soviet economy focused on investment in more butter and thus in fewer guns.

More negative interpretations of U.S. policy, often credited to unnamed U.S. officials ("a high-ranking intelligence officer" is a favorite here), imply that the United States is not merely pessimistic about chances of a Soviet pullout but does not want one. This line holds that the United States is prepared to "fight to the last Afghan" because of what the war is doing to Soviet prestige worldwide. The USSR is pictured as a nation that is honestly seeking a way out of its impasse, as witness its continued willingness to discuss withdrawal with UN Undersecretary General Diego Cordovez in Geneva, but is being frustrated by U.S. machinations. Periodic optimistic reports, indicating agreement has all but been reached on a peaceful solution, seem intended to induce a wishful Pavlovian reaction among those who want peace—and rage when that reward is denied them.[26] The accusation that the United States is sabotaging negotiations ignores the fact that, moral grounds aside, the U.S. has a vested interest in promoting a Soviet withdrawal in order to remove the strategic threat to the Persian Gulf that the Soviet presence in Afghanistan poses.

Another line holds that the Soviet Union is actually pleased with a chance to blood its troops and test its equipment in Afghanistan, that it is confident of eventual victory, and that it can continue to suffer the losses of the past five years indefinitely. This is undoubtedly a genuinely felt emotion among a set of Soviet military officers but is not necessarily representative of Soviet thinking at large. As a way of projecting confidence, however, it has merit for the Soviet cause.

Moreover, the USSR is allegedly exercising "restraint" by not exploiting Baluch separatism in order to destabilize Pakistan, a tactic it supposedly could employ at any time. The implication is that the noncommunist world should accept a settlement on Soviet terms before Moscow's patience runs out.[27] In fact, the USSR has consistently tried to fan Baluch separatism, either directly or via Afghan surrogates, since the 1920s. In recent times, a combination of Pakistani efforts to adopt a more understanding attitude toward its Baluch minority and the Soviet incursion into Afghanistan have combined to blunt the thrust of separatism; far from being a net exporter of revolution into Baluchistan, the DRA has become an unwilling importer.[28]

Particularly in 1984, there has been an effort to convince audiences outside as well as inside Afghanistan that the backbone of the resistance has been broken, and that Babrak Karmal, "a moderate communist," is earning the grudging respect of even noncommunist Afghans and is progressively extending the area of DRA control over the countryside. Parallel to this is a picture of the mujahideen (again credited to unnamed noncommunist Afghans and/or Pakistanis) as divided, unscrupulous, willing to inform Soviet forces of impending attacks by rival groups, obscurantist, medieval, and deserting in ever greater numbers to the DRA side.[29] In fact, as shown in the previous chapter, the DRA and USSR are, if anything, in even worse disarray in coping with the resistance than they were a year ago, whereas the resistance is expanding its modest political infrastructure inside Afghanistan and coordinating its military operations to an ever greater degree.

Effects in the "Second World"

At the start of this chapter we examined the reactions to the Soviet invasion by the "First World," i.e., the United States and other developed noncommunist countries, as well as the reactions of the Third World. What of the "Second World," the USSR and its allies?

The initial reaction within the Warsaw Pact and its ideological affiliates was an obedient echoing of Moscow's line by all but Romania, which initially maintained a discreet silence. Before the end of 1980, however, President Nicolae Ceauşescu publicly called for the USSR to withdraw its troops, whereas Poland and Hungary let the USSR know their opinion that the invasion had been a "serious and damaging mistake."[30] Subsequent developments in Poland, including the rise of Solidarity and the failure of the USSR to intervene militarily there, were certainly influenced by Afghan developments. The community of interest shared among Afghans and Poles in their resistance to Soviet hegemony—and the historic significance of that resistance—has been emphasized by the Polish intellectual Aleksander Smolar.[31]

Meanwhile, West European Communist parties either broke with Moscow over the invasion (as in the case of the Italian party) or suffered humiliating defeats at the polls (as happened to the French). It is significant that before they took posts in Mitterrand's Socialist cabinet in 1981, four Communist ministers felt obliged to issue a statement in favor of Afghan self-determination and for a withdrawal of Soviet troops.[32] In recent times, Soviet support for small, hard-core splinter groups in West European parties has been observed. This may signal Soviet rejection of the legal, parliamentary track taken by those parties in the post-Stalin era and a reversion to the disciplined, conspiratorial, and, if necessary, illegal approaches pursued in the early days of the communist movement. If so, the dispute over Afghanistan will have been one of the issues that led to that decision.

Regardless of effects outside the USSR, conventional wisdom holds that the Kremlin need have no concern about the impact of Soviet public opinion on its foreign policy decisionmaking. Unpopular domestic policies in the USSR occasionally can meet with determined and even public resistance, but in foreign affairs the harshest Soviet critics tend to accept the official siege mentality that sees the USSR under perpetual threat of attack from outside enemies. Soviet propaganda successfully exploits and intensifies an innate national paranoia bred of the wars and invasions suffered by Russians in this and previous centuries.

Nevertheless, the USSR has now been engaged militarily in Afghanistan for longer than its participation in World War II. The casualties are minimal compared to those of 1941–1945, but they are significant and perhaps even more painful for surviving relatives: in this case, unlike the Great Patriotic War, there is no believable threat to the homeland involved. Moreover, with the rotation of troops through Afghanistan tens of thousands of eyewitnesses are returning to give firsthand reports of the situation in that country.

Increasing numbers of Soviet prisoners of war and army defectors have cut even further into Soviet prestige. A few have even converted to Islam and joined the resistance as active fighters, while others have said they do not want to be repatriated. As an experiment, the International Red Cross arranged to hold eight (later eleven) POWs at a minimum security jail in Switzerland for two years on the understanding that an equal number of mujahideen prisoners would be released in their custody. The Soviet side never fulfilled its obligation, and one of the Soviet POWs succeeded in escaping to Germany, where he received political asylum. Two of three others whose two-year term expired on May 20, 1984, refused repatriation and were granted political asylum in Switzerland. As of late 1984, the Red Cross program appears to be moribund, but meanwhile a private organization to aid Soviet defectors, Count Tolstoy's Soviet Prisoners Afghan Rescue Committee, has been resettling in Europe those defectors and POWs who do not want to return to the USSR.[33]

Although the number of Soviet soldiers on active duty with the mujahideen remains small, rumors are already spreading in Pakistan as well as among the Soviet occupation forces that an all-Soviet anticommunist fighting unit is forming or has been formed. Even in rumor form, such reports must haunt those Kremlin leaders old enough to remember the Vlasov movement, the World War II alliance of former Soviet citizens eager to become allies of Germany to overthrow Stalin. The problem of defecting troops has been chronic for Russian and Soviet troops throughout history.[34]

One of the more astonishing and courageous feats of protest inside the USSR was that of Vladimir Danchev, an English-language announcer for Radio Moscow who gave two broadcasts on May 18 and three more on May 23, 1983, in which he applied to Soviet troops all the pejorative adjectives Moscow normally uses in connection with the mujahideen.[35] Perhaps the most revealing part of the story was that no one in Moscow detected the difference until British reporters asked questions and Soviet authorities played over the tapes. Danchev was then removed, but meanwhile it had been conclusively demonstrated that Soviet citizens are all but deaf to their own propaganda, at least in English.

In recent times several scholars of East European affairs (most notably R. V. Burks of Wayne State University) have raised serious questions about the long-term stability of the USSR. The "political landslides" (i.e., popular, spontaneous anticommunist revolts) that have taken place in East Germany, Hungary, Czechoslovakia, and Poland in recent decades are acknowledged as more likely to occur in those satellite countries than in the Soviet motherland, but a persuasive case has been made that the phenomenon is possible and even probable in the USSR itself. If this is so, the significance of Afghanistan could be critical. As another scholar has written,

> The days of muddling through while the vast majority of the Soviet people quietly acquiesces may be coming to an end. Significant change is perhaps becoming more likely. The gap between propaganda and reality in Afghanistan, and the likely negative effect of this on Soviet public opinion, might well make an important contribution to the coming changes.[36]

CHAPTER

11

US Policy:
Before and After

*Failure to understand the Soviet Union is the principal
cause of its successes*

(French political scientist and
historian Alain Besançon)[1]

Could the United States have prevented the events that led to the
Soviet invasion and occupation? Now that it has happened, is it irreversible? If not, what U.S. policies would best serve to induce a
withdrawal? If the Soviets cannot be dislodged, what policies might
deter them from similar encroachments elsewhere?

Pre-invasion U.S. Policy Options

In trying to answer the first of these questions one must distinguish
between the period prior to the communist coup of April 1978 and the
Taraki-Amin era of 1978–1979, when the United States had lost most
of its leverage in the country. It is also necessary to put Afghanistan in
context with various perceptions of the worldwide balance of forces,
with political developments in the USSR, and with the United States'
neo-isolationism of the late 1970s.

As noted in the last chapter, by 1979 the growing might of the Soviet
military machine had lent a self-confidence and aggressiveness to
Kremlin planners unparalleled in modern times. At the same time the
United States foreign policy seemed adrift, the country's unmatched
national power shackled by an electorate still haunted by the Vietnam
tragedy. The apparent helplessness of the U.S. giant when Iranian
students first seized the entire American Embassy staff in Teheran and
then held it hostage with impunity for week after week was painfully

symbolic, and the symbolism was not lost on those watching from the Kremlin.

Had the USSR been in the position of the United States, it almost surely would have made an immediate and decisive military thrust to rescue the hostages, even at the risk of innocent lives and with the certain opprobrium of most of the world. American failure to respond in this fashion sent a signal to the Soviet leaders that they need have no fear of an armed response by the U.S. to their Afghan adventure. This is not to suggest that such a thrust was definitely called for (too many other factors entered into that decisionmaking equation) nor to claim that the USSR would have been deterred from making its attack. Nevertheless, a resolute American show of force unquestionably would have affected Kremlin deliberations. Military activity in the region by U.S. forces might well have carried dangers of confrontation unacceptable to the Soviet leaders. It may be significant that the final decision to invade allegedly was made at the end of November, some three weeks after the hostages were seized and when it was already obvious that the Americans were not going to move.[2]

In retrospect it is clear that as the 1970s drew to a close the region was fated for violence, and it is doubtful that any action by the United States would have done more than delay the invasion. Over decades the progressively greater Soviet investment and commitment in Afghanistan—first economic, then political, and finally quasi-military (as advisors and pilots were drawn into combat)—made it more and more awkward for Moscow to retreat. On the Afghan side, the mujahideen were ever more popular and the DRA was ever more politically bankrupt. For the USSR the choice was between humiliating retreat or a quantum jump in their investment. To the cocksure Soviet generals, that was no choice at all.

Before the April 1978 coup, however, the Soviet commitment had been relatively light. If that coup had failed, the USSR would have shrugged off its losses, disavowed Abdul Qader and his colleagues as a group of disgruntled, apolitical military officers (perhaps with CIA connections), and begun building for the next opportunity. It is virtually certain that there would have been no military intervention to support the PDPA or to free its jailed leaders at that time. For the United States, the time to have taken preventive measures was before the coup; thereafter, most options were closed and the Soviet commitment became increasingly difficult to reverse.

During Daoud's 1973–1978 stewardship of Afghanistan, U.S. policies were by and large the best that could have been applied, given the political climate in Kabul and the lack of domestic American enthusiasm for foreign involvements. Our aid projects, although severely restricted in comparison with those of earlier years, were long-term and generally successful, including a little-known but widely appreciated textbook program for primary and secondary schools. Had we been in a position to increase aid dramatically (without a corresponding willingness to undertake strategic commitments in the country), it probably would only have provoked the USSR into moving against Daoud even earlier.

One of the key developments that preceded the 1978 coup, however, was the reconciliation in mid-1977 between the Parcham and Khalq factions of the PDPA. That should have sounded warning bells in Washington, for it should have been obvious to analysts of Afghanistan that this was no freely achieved political compromise in the Western sense of politics, but an imposed union that overrode deep-seated antagonisms. Only one outside force could have predominated over the mutual distrust that Parcham and Khalq felt for one another: the fount of ideology to which they both owed allegiance, the CPSU. If that fact had been recognized, then an estimate should have been made concerning the reconciliation's significance in terms of Soviet intentions. If nothing else there should have been an intensified effort by U.S. observers in Afghanistan to determine what the newly unified PDPA was up to.

Assuming that the information had been acquired and correctly assessed, and that a recommendation for action had been made, what theoretical options were open to Washington? In earlier years the United States might have considered setting up or supporting some kind of counterforce inside Afghanistan to offset the growing threat from the left; or it might have increased foreign aid sharply in an attempt to alleviate the dissatisfactions that gave the left new adherents. Neither of these would have been a viable option in the late 1970s. Foreign aid was increasingly difficult to obtain from the American Congress, and "meddling in internal affairs" of foreign lands had become extremely unpopular among the American electorate.

The only counterforce that could have thwarted the PDPA was Daoud himself. If we did have the information (and we should have had it), and if we did assess it correctly (as we should have), some way should have been devised to put into Daoud's hands the full benefit of our information and analysis without compromising the means by which they were acquired. Daoud was a suspicious man who held no love for the United States, but he was also known to be concerned about the PDPA even before it refused to merge with his single-party system and to support the 1977 constitution. Had the United States set up a discreet liaison arrangement with him in good time, it is possible that he could have forestalled the April 1978 coup.

Once the coup had taken place, U.S. options were severely restricted. The temptation to provide military support to Afghan insurgents who were fighting the Taraki and Amin regimes was resisted. This withholding of aid was painful but it was the correct decision in light of the subsequent developments. Had there been such U.S. support, there would have been a significant body of opinion in the United States and throughout the world that U.S. "meddling" had prompted and justified the Soviet invasion, as indeed Soviet propaganda has tried so hard to convince the world ever since. In such circumstances, our own determination to take countermeasures after the invasion would also have been severely weakened.[3]

Nevertheless, restricted though U.S. options were, there is cause for concern in our failure to react effectively to obvious Soviet preparations for invasion until those preparations had reached an irreversible stage. There were some muted indications of such a move as early as mid-1979, and clearer evidence emerged in September, just before Taraki returned from Moscow to meet death at Amin's hands. According to subsequent accounts, the United States delivered to the USSR no fewer than five warnings against invasion, but that was during the last weeks of 1979, too late to be effective. Only the December 22 warning was made public at the time and Soviet preparations went ahead undeterred. To hold the first warning confidential might have been warranted, but thenceforth, late as it was, the United States should have focused world attention on the Soviet preparations and started to mobilize international opposition to it.

Degree of Soviet Commitment

Whether any move or combination of moves could have averted the invasion is a matter for historical guesswork. Of more immediate importance is whether the decision to sweep Afghanistan into the

Soviet dominion by force was then, is now, and forever will be considered irreversible by the Kremlin. In judging this question there is an unfortunate penchant of many analysts to overestimate both Soviet capabilities and Soviet intentions. Worse, they often seem to suffer from an unforgivable confusion between the two, reflected in the apparent belief that just because the USSR has set its mind on a goal, it will achieve that goal.

Conventional wisdom says the USSR is in Afghanistan to stay, and the rest of the world had better accommodate to that unpleasant reality. Persons who advocate this position point out that those rare occasions when the USSR has voluntarily withdrawn occupation troops, such as from northern Iran in 1946 and from Austria in 1955, were neither typical nor comparable to Afghanistan today. Much more apt, they say, is the analogy with Mongolia, a Soviet protectorate even more tightly bound to Moscow than the countries of Eastern Europe. They forecast a permanent Soviet presence in Afghanistan, an occupation for which Moscow can be made to pay dearly but not one subject to negotiation or unilateral revocation.[4]

On the surface their arguments are persuasive. Although the costs of invasion and occupation unquestionably have been higher than originally anticipated by the Kremlin, the price of retreat still appears to be even greater than the continuing drain of men, matériel, and prestige. This price includes the potential spread of Islamic nationalist contagion into Soviet Central Asia and the weakening of the Soviet hold on Eastern Europe, as well as the surrender of a strategically valuable stepping-stone toward domination of Middle East oil resources. The argument overlooks, however, the fact that the USSR is already paying those prices to a significant degree: Central Asians are awakening to the fact that the Afghans are not giving up; in Eastern Europe growing political restlessness is fueled in part by the mujahideen's heroic fight; and in no way can Afghanistan be considered a safe stepping-stone to anywhere so long as the resistance controls most of the country. The question for Moscow's leaders is, as it was for the United States in Vietnam, at what point to accept the penalties of humiliating defeat in one small area of operations in order to avoid even more serious and far-reaching losses. That point has not yet been reached, but those who claim it does not exist are unconsciously and needlessly restricting U.S. policy options.

Many of these analysts are the same ones who predicted so confidently in 1980 that the invasion would destroy the resistance "immediately," and, when that did not happen, pushed the date to "when the snows melt," "when the [summer 1980] Olympics are over," "when the harvest is in," and finally "when the snows come." The fact that none of these predictions came true has not deterred the analysts from projecting their gloomy forecasts into a more distant future, now prudently far enough ahead in time for them to avoid embarrassment if proven wrong. Aside from running the danger of becoming a self-fulfilling prophecy (voicing such beliefs has a pernicious effect on the willingness of persons inside and outside Afghanistan to persevere in the anti-Soviet struggle), such predictions ignore some very important indications that the USSR is not totally and forever committed to its Afghan adventure.

Granted, there are no signs today that the Soviets are seriously contemplating withdrawal in the near future. The cat-and-mouse game being played with the UN's Diego Cordovez for a "political solution" is designed more to project an image of Soviet sincerity to the world than to achieve the proclaimed goal of withdrawal. This said, it is most important to emphasize that *the Kremlin leaders since before their invasion have prudently left the door open for a retreat if it should become necessary.*

As noted previously, Afghanistan is *no longer* considered a member of the "socialist family of nations," only having enjoyed that exalted designation in the Soviet press for a brief period in early 1979 and in the Afghan press from a few months after the 1978 coup until the invasion. Thereafter the country reverted to the "national democratic" category, the designation the PDPA assigned itself from 1966 to 1978. This retrogression is most unusual if not unique in communist annals. Not only are the words *socialist* and *socialism* rigorously excluded from any discussion of present-day party or state developments in the official Afghan media, they are not even forecast as a goal to be achieved in the future. Whatever other reasons might exist for this backpedaling, its significance here is that the USSR is no longer bound in Afghanistan by the Brezhnev Doctrine (the obligation to defend socialism, by force of arms if necessary, anywhere in the world that it is threatened). *In short, there is no ideological imperative to protect Afghan socialism because, according to Moscow, Afghan socialism does not exist.*

On the state level, it is significant that the USSR has held consistently to its line that the "limited military contingents" would be withdrawn as soon as all forms of "outside interference" in the country ceased. Whether or not that interference actually exists is immaterial; the war can be declared won at any time, particularly because Afghanistan is not a member of the Warsaw Pact. Although the 1978 Friendship Treaty provides for the possibility of armed assistance (in fact the USSR has justified its invasion in part by that treaty), such intervention is voluntary, not obligatory, as it would be if the DRA held Warsaw Pact membership. Afghanistan is not even a member of Comecon, though it enjoys observer status with that group. *Thus, there is no governmental obligation for the USSR to protect the DRA either.*

(Note here the contrast with Mongolia, which, though still a backward country, is a member of both the Warsaw Pact and Comecon, and is termed in the communist press to be "on the road to socialism," even if not very far along it.)

To be sure, the USSR has made it very clear that it considers the Afghan revolution to be "irreversible." Moreover, the Soviet troops there are said to be doing their "internationalist duty." In this and other formulations there is a strong element of implied ideological commitment, just as the Soviet government's vociferous support of the DRA signals implicit commitment on the state level. Nevertheless, so long as these commitments remain nonexplicit, they are not binding.

Just because of that fact's enormous implications, it is impossible to believe that the absence of firm Soviet guarantees is accidental. With only a few strokes of the pen, Afghanistan could be placed in Mongolia's status, a move that would have a considerable psychological impact, if not on the Afghan mujahideen (who would fight on no matter how the USSR related to them) then on their supporters in the West. Many who advocate aid to the resistance because they detect the possibility of an eventual Soviet withdrawal might have second thoughts if they believed the mujahideen cause to be hopeless. Moscow's failure to dress Afghanistan formally in socialist and Warsaw Pact robes can be taken as a sign that, however gloomy others may be, the Kremlin does not discount the possibility that the resistance might eventually triumph. It would be foolish and needlessly limiting for the U.S. government to write off Afghanistan as firmly and forever in the Soviet camp when not even the USSR itself has dared to make that claim unequivocally.

Soviet Political Divisions

If there is eventually to be a Soviet withdrawal, it will not be due solely to the spirited resistance, even though that will be a major contributing factor. The economic dislocations, social unrest, and political instability that threaten not only Eastern Europe but the very Soviet heartland will weigh more heavily than the actual fighting in Afghanistan. Meanwhile, due to the upheavals in connection with successive leadership changes in Moscow, it is now the USSR that gives the impression of being adrift, unable to project innovative policies at home or abroad. In order to visualize a set of circumstances under which some new leader might undertake the voluntary withdrawal of Soviet troops, it is necessary to take a brief look at the shifting interrelationship between the three major sources of political power in the USSR: the CPSU, the military, and the secret police (today's KGB).

Under Stalin, the secret police reigned supreme. On his death, the party conspired with the military and physically did away with secret-police chief Lavrentiy Beria, sharply downgrading his ministry-level apparatus to a simple "Committee of State Security attached to the Council of Ministers." Once Khrushchev had secured his own position as undisputed party chief, he turned on the military, and it was the party that held unchallenged power.

Later, Khrushchev's ouster was arranged by his disgruntled party subordinates with the tacit consent (and to the grim satisfaction) of the military and KGB. Under his successor, Leonid Brezhnev, the party initially continued to run the country, but it was rotting from within. Well before the end of Brezhnev's long reign, the military and KGB, in quiet collusion, were influencing policy to an ever greater degree, as witness the Afghan invasion and other projections of military power abroad (Angola, Ethiopia, and South Yemen). Thus, when Brezhnev died in late 1982, it was not too surprising that his chosen successor, Konstantin Chernenko, was passed over in favor of KGB chief Yuriy Andropov, nor were the subsequent purges that afflicted the party unexpected.

Before Andropov could get well into the saddle, however, physical infirmities carried him off. Even during his short reign there were signs that the military-KGB alliance might be starting to break down, and it was the military that now was starting to emerge as the dominant force. Andropov's death came before that struggle was resolved, and Chernenko was retrieved from obscurity to take over as symbolic chief while others fought for real power behind the scenes. As of mid-1984 the outcome is still in doubt, but it is not unlikely that a new coalition between weaker forces—now the KGB and the party—is trying to undermine the leading group, the military. Their chances of success are problematical, but if they do not succeed today, history indicates they might well do so tomorrow.

In such a situation, a new leader untainted by the decision to invade Afghanistan would be in a position to undertake dramatic ways of restoring momentum to Soviet society, especially if domestic problems become overwhelming. Withdrawing the occupation forces would be one such move. It would result in huge economic savings, an improvement in the USSR's image abroad, and great popularity for him among Soviet conscripts and their close relations (to say nothing of their counterparts in Afghanistan). Not least important, it could serve to discredit his predecessors and current rivals of an older generation, a need that seems to be felt by each successive Soviet leader.

Such a scenario may be visionary, but it is not impossible. Countless variations and alternatives exist, but if one thing seems certain it is that the trickling, exasperating hemorrhage of Soviet resources caused by the Afghan adventure, though bearable in the short term, cannot go on indefinitely. The choices are between an ultimately successful Soviet pacification of the country or a Soviet retreat. And that choice, at least in part, depends on the United States.

U.S. Policy Options

Paradoxically, the Soviet invasion actually broadened U.S. policy options in Afghanistan. The precedent of intervention having been set by the USSR's unprovoked attack, the question of other foreign involvement became much less sensitive. The basic problem was no longer whether but how to aid the mujahideen. Unsettled situations in Pakistan and Iran, however—the only two countries through which aid could reach the resistance—posed daunting physical and political problems. (China, Afghanistan's other neighbor, has only a very short border in an inaccessible area that Soviet troops have succeeded in largely sealing off.)

Iran's Islamic fundamentalist revolution has effectively denied Iranian territory to the United States for any purpose. Though opposing the Soviet invasion, the Iranians have been, if anything, less bitterly antagonistic to the USSR than to America, which has continued to head their list of demon nations. Moreover, they have been tied down with their war against Iraq for almost as long as the USSR has been fighting in Afghanistan. They have given some aid and comfort to mujahideen from northern and western Afghanistan, especially fellow Shiite Muslims, but Afghan refugees in Iran have been generally worse off than those who have escaped to Pakistan. Moreover, there are reports of some Afghan refugees being drafted to fight the Iraqis. If the Iran-Iraq war winds down and if the fundamentalist fanaticism of the Khomeini government eases, it might be possible for aid under the aegis of another Islamic power to be channeled to Afghanistan via Iran, but as of mid-1984 that prospect appears remote.

This leaves Pakistan, which poses its own peculiar set of thorny problems. U.S. relations with the government of General Mohammed Zia-ul-Haq have been complicated by his human rights record, by the apparent intent of Pakistan to develop a nuclear weapons capability, and by the necessity for the United States to maintain some balance in its relations with Pakistan and India. Most basically, however, the U.S. problem is one of credibility: will Washington stand by an ally in distress? Unfortunately, the record of American inconsistency is not one to lend great confidence to leaders in other countries.

The question is critical, because if reported U.S. interest in helping the mujahideen falters for any reason, Pakistan—over whose territory the arms have flowed—will be left defenseless to face an angry and unrestrained Russian bear. Even today, the USSR can (and almost certainly does) threaten to increase various destabilizing measures that it already pursues, from encouraging Baluch separatism to supporting Pakistan's pro-Soviet National Awami Party to lending support to Pakistan's arch-rival, India. These real or implicit threats inhibit Pakistan from allowing unlimited arms aid to the mujahideen to funnel through the country. In fact, in the eyes of many, Pakistani restrictions have held both the quantity and quality of weapons delivered to the resistance to an unacceptably low level.

Some Pakistani doubts on the degree of U.S. commitment were put to rest in 1981 when President Reagan raised the previous administration's suggested aid package from $200 million over two years ("Peanuts," had been Zia's scornful response to that offer) to $3.2 billion. Half of the aid was to be military, half economic. Although this demonstrated the good faith of the U.S. government's executive branch, it did not necessarily constitute a blessing from the entire U.S. government, nor was it guaranteed to extend beyond the next presidential election, three years hence. What was needed—and still is needed in mid-1984—*is clear and unmistakable bipartisan support from the entire U.S. government for the national liberation of Afghanistan.* This does not imply commitment of U.S. forces to that end (nor should there ever be such a commitment), but it does carry with it an obligation to deliver an adequate supply of adequate weapons on a continuing basis to the mujahideen—and, by implication, to safeguard the routes by which those arms reach their destination, i.e., Pakistan.

A joint resolution calling for increased arms aid to the mujahideen was initiated in Congress in 1982. Over two years later, after delays apparently caused by domestic and international pressures, it was put to a vote and passed overwhelmingly.[5] How much of the delay can be laid to the Pakistanis' own concerns about possibly provoking the Russians and how much to other U.S. policy considerations is unclear.

In any case, now that a firm, bipartisan American position on aid appears to have been established, it should become possible to remove some of the hobbles for which Pakistani trepidations (presumably) have been responsible: insistence that the aid be supplied covertly, that it consist only of Soviet-model matériel, and that it come only in small quantities. It may be in U.S. interests to retain a measure of secrecy about the extent and composition of arms aid, but there should be no inhibitions in providing more and better-quality weapons and munitions than have been sent so far.[6] Specifically, modern hand-held antitank and antiaircraft missiles of Western make, such as the U.S. Stinger, should find their way into Afghan hands. (The fact that these have been made available to Saudi Arabia provides a convenient rationale for their arrival in Afghanistan, should the covert nature of the aid be a requirement.) Better light mortars and other infantry weapons, perhaps those developed for mountain troops in Italy, Switzerland, and Austria, should be made available.

Moreover, aid should transcend the military:

1. Medicine, medical equipment, and advice on sanitation are urgent requirements, not only in Pakistan among the refugees but inside Afghanistan itself.

2. Agricultural advice and food are needed as the Soviets try to depopulate the countryside and destroy the resistance's support structure.

3. School supplies, from pencils and paper to advanced textbooks, should be provided to encourage establishment of noncommunist schools.

4. Instruction on local government, to help the resistance set up its own political infrastructure, is needed.

5. Media equipment, from light printing presses to small radio broadcasting stations, are reportedly available to some degree but perhaps could be upgraded. Although the literacy rate remains low, "night letters" (*shabnamah*, clandestinely distributed leaflets) are a classic Afghan way of registering dissent.

These actions would help establish the resistance not only as a fighting force but as an alternative government. A more problematic question is whether the United States should try to heal the splits among the various mutually antagonistic Afghan resistance groups and the Pakistan-based emigrés. Unlike Parcham and Khalq, none of these owes allegiance to any foreign power; in fact some are almost as hostile to the United States as to the Soviet Union. Our ability to exert leverage, even if that were desirable, is severely circumscribed.

On the other hand, the military and political capabilities of the resistance are badly weakened by the continued bickering among the various groups, which is indubitably encouraged clandestinely by the PDPA and by the Soviet and PDPA agents who have penetrated them. The United States should set as an intelligence goal the identification and public exposure of hostile agents in the emigration, at the same time discouraging factionalism of all kinds—even if not provoked by Communists—by hammering home the theme that divisiveness is a Soviet tactic. Until the day comes that some charismatic leader can forge a measure of Afghan unity in the resistance, however, the United

States should take only a passive, advisory role in promoting union, while exposing all who would prevent it.

Still another option for the United States is an intensified information effort: to make the world aware to the fullest degree and in the most timely fashion of developments in Afghanistan. This means declassifying and making public current intelligence about the country. Intended audiences should include not only the Third World and Western Europe but particularly the USSR and the Afghans themselves.

The most important feature missing from coverage of Afghanistan today is immediacy. In tandem with broadcasting equipment for resistance-operated stations like Radio Free Kabul to local audiences, there should be transmitters powerful enough to reach the outside world so that live-coverage broadcasts can be heard internationally. (Russian or Central Asian announcers from the emigré community should be used to beam these directly to the Soviet audiences across the border as well as to the occupation troops.) Even better, if technically feasible, would be live or on-the-scenes videotaped television coverage of Afghan developments, relayed by satellite and bringing the war into the world's living rooms on a real-time basis.

The pressure on the Soviet Union to leave Afghanistan should be sustained and unrelenting. It should be White House policy to repeat on a regular basis our support for the Afghan resistance and our condemnation of the continued Soviet occupation. Moscow counts on the United States' short political attention span to relieve any pressure we might try to exert, and it must be demonstrated to them that in this case we will not let up.

There are those who argue that the USSR cannot afford to appear to give in to U.S. pressure, and that we ought provide a "graceful escape route" for them. The USSR, however, has shown an ability in the past to put on any given Soviet act whatever interpretation it feels is appropriate. The very invasion of Afghanistan is a case in point. If it decides to pull out of the country, it will need no "ladder" of our manufacture. Although it may be in U.S. interests to vary the degree of pressure we exert from time to time (and perhaps to promise a respite in return for real progress on a Soviet withdrawal), we should not feel obliged to concern ourselves with Soviet sensitivities to an excessive degree.

At the same time we should also disabuse the USSR of any fears that a vengeful Afghanistan, with or without U.S. support, will become its blood enemy and attempt to stir up trouble in Soviet Central Asia. The Afghans cannot afford to have bad relations with the USSR, any more than they could afford bad relations with Britain before 1947. The Soviets might be reminded that the Afghans always adhered strictly to the neutrality guarantees they had given the British, even when the latter were in desperate straits (e.g., during the Indian mutiny of 1857, World War I, and World War II).

Finally, we as a government should make it abundantly clear to everyone — Afghans, Soviets, and the rest of the world — that we have no intention whatsoever of supplanting the USSR as Afghanistan's "big brother" or of managing its affairs. The United States has no interest in seeing Afghanistan revert to anything but its traditional role as a nationally free, truly nonaligned, and independent country.

It is all too easy to come up with recommendations like the foregoing and feel that the job has been done. The United States government has now been advised how to proceed and the rest of us can sit back and monitor how well our representatives perform. But it is not only the U.S. government that has an obligation here; every person of every nationality who believes in individual freedom, national self-determination, and the preservation of cultural heritage has a duty to support the Afghan resistance however he can. In a very real way the mujahideen, in their own minds fighting only for their own freedom, are fighting for everyone else's as well.

Western opinion molders have an especially important duty to keep the Afghan issue alive and reported accurately. In the United States few are doing the job well. When reported on at all the mujahideen are called "rebels." Were the French Maquis rebels? The Norwegian underground? The Soviet partisans? Yet the Nazi invasions and occupations that gave birth to those movements were no more alien than what the USSR has inflicted on Afghanistan, and the mujahideen resistance today is no less legitimate an expression of national will than the various resistances in Europe were then. The Afghan story needs to be told and retold. Journalists, photographers, and radio announcers need to be sent in with the mujahideen, their copy should be transmitted on a timely basis to the outside world, and the final product must be featured prominently.

In the final analysis, the question of whether the Afghans win or lose will be decided by how many people feel that the mujahideen struggle is their own and hence decide to help. If the rest of the world turns its back and Soviet arms ultimately prevail, no person or nation who ignored that fight will have a justifiable complaint if and when Soviet arms eventually are turned on them.

Notes

Chapter 1

1. Quoted in A. Evelyn Ashley, *The Life of Lord Palmerston*, vol. 2 (London: R. Bentley and Son, 1876), p. 25. Cited in Vartan Gregorian, *The Emergence of Modern Afghanistan* (Stanford: Stanford University Press, 1969), p. 102.

2. Abdur Rahman Khan, *The Life of Abdur Rahman Khan, Amir of Afghanistan*, vol. 2, ed. Sultan Mohammed Khan (London: J. Murray, 1900), p. 280. Quoted in Louis Dupree, *Afghanistan* (Princeton: Princeton University Press, 1973), p. 415.

3. Gregorian, *Modern Afghanistan*, p. 132.

4. Ibid, pp. 203–4.

5. Ibid.

6. A. C. Jewett, *An American Engineer in Afghanistan*, ed. Marjorie Jewett Bell (Minneapolis: University of Minnesota Press, 1948), pp. 303ff. See also Gregorian, *Modern Afghanistan*, p. 205.

7. Gregorian, *Modern Afghanistan*, p. 220. The characterization of the three factions is his.

8. Ibid., p. 226.

9. *Kabul Times*, August 3, 1978.

10. Ibid., August 7, 1978.

11. Gregorian, *Modern Afghanistan*, p. 226. The original source is listed as "The War in Afghanistan," *Labour Monthly* 2, no. 3 (March 1929): 181.

Chapter 2

1. V. M. Vinogradov et al., eds., *Sovetsko-afganskiye otnosheniya, 1919–1969*, (Moscow: Politizdat, 1971), p. 7.

2. Ibid., pp. 11–12.

3. Ibid., pp. 8–9.

4. Ibid., pp. 10–11.

5. Vartan Gregorian, *The Emergence of Modern Afghanistan* (Stanford: Stanford University Press, 1969), p. 232.

6. Y. Volkov et al., *The Truth About Afghanistan: Documents, Facts, Eyewitness Reports* (Moscow: Novosti Press Agency Publishing House, 1980), p. 23.

7. Georges Agabekov, *OGPU: The Russian Secret Terror* (New York: Brentanos, 1931), p. 46. Agabekov personally carried the first million rubles to Kabul in 1924.

8. Vinogradov et al., *Sovetsko-afganskiye otnosheniya*, pp. 11–12.

9. Gregorian, *Modern Afghanistan*, p. 474.

10. Ibid., pp. 235, 474.

11. Ibid., p. 232. Gregorian is citing Louis Fischer, *The Soviets in World Affairs*, vol. 1 (London: J. Cape, 1930), p. 286.

12. S. I. Ozhegov, *Slovar' russkogo yazyka*, 10th ed. (Moscow: Izdatel'stvo "Sovetskaya Entsiklopediya," 1973).

13. Yu. A. Polyakov and A. I. Chugunov, *Konets basmachestva* (Moscow: Nauka, 1976), p. 3.

14. Hélène Carrère d'Encausse, *L'Empire éclaté* (Paris: Flammarion, 1978), p. 26.

15. Polyakov and Chugunov, *Konets basmachestva*, p. 44.

16. Ibid., pp. 79–80, 84, and 127–28, for example. Soviet authors have no reason to emphasize such matters, but are clearly aggrieved by the duplicity of the locals.

17. *San Francisco Chronicle*, September 3, 1980.

18. Polyakov and Chugunov, *Konets basmachestva*, pp. 93–95.

19. Ibid., p. 55.

20. Gregorian, *Modern Afghanistan*, p. 232.

21. Ibid.

22. Polyakov and Chugunov, *Konets basmachestva*, p. 67.

23. Ibid., p. 90.

24. Ibid., pp. 70–71.

25. Fitzroy MacLean, *Eastern Approaches* (London: J. Cape, 1949), p. 146; and Robert Conquest, *The Great Terror* (New York: Macmillan, 1968), pp. 516–19.

26. Polyakov and Chugunov, *Konets basmachestva*, p. 101.

27. Volkov et al., *The Truth About Afghanistan*, p. 24.

28. Polyakov and Chugunov, *Konets basmachestva*, pp. 40, 168–69.

29. Ibid., pp. 93–94.

30. Vinogradov et al., *Sovetsko-afganskiye otnosheniya*, p. 29.

31. Guenther Nollau and Hans Juergen Wiehe, *Russia's South Flank* (New York: Praeger, 1963), p. 98.

32. Ibid., p. 101.

33. Gregorian, *Modern Afghanistan*, p. 238.

34. Ibid.

35. Ibid., p. 255, and Louis Dupree, *Mahmud Tarzi: Forgotten Nationalist*, American Universities Field Staff Report (AUFS) South Asia Series, vol. 8, no. 1, January 1964, LD–1–64, p. 2.

36. Louis Dupree, *Afghanistan's "Big Gamble," Part I: Historical Background of Afghan-Russian Relations*, American Universities Field Staff Report (AUFS), South Asia Series, vol. 4, no. 3, April 1960, LD–3–60, p. 13.

37. Vinogradov et al., *Sovetsko-afganskiye otnosheniya*, p. 45.

38. Polyakov and Chugunov, *Konets basmachestva*, p. 131.

39. Agabekov, *OGPU*, pp. 86–93.

40. Dupree, *Afghanistan's "Big Gamble" Part I*, AUFS, LD–3–60, p. 13.

41. Agabekov, *OGPU*, pp. 158–70; and Gregorian, *Modern Afghanistan*, pp. 278–79. The sources are divided on the question of whether Ghulam Nabi's forces were defeated in the field or whether they voluntarily withdrew from a militarily winning position because of Amanullah's abdication.

42. Polyakov and Chugunov, *Konets basmachestva*, pp. 138–39. The Soviet authors of course also lay a good deal of blame for the Basmachi on foreign intrigues, but it is obvious that Afghanistan was too beset with domestic problems for such meddling, while Britain, with the onset of the depression, was scarcely in a position to foment rebellion so far from home.

43. Ibid., p. 164.

44. Dupree, *Afghanistan's "Big Gamble": Part I*, AUFS, LD–3–60, p. 14.

45. Gregorian, *Modern Afghanistan*, p. 338.

46. Agabekov, *OGPU*, pp. 86–93.

47. An uncertain but intriguing indicator of possible clandestine Soviet con-

nections with Ghulam Nabi is provided by recent Afghan historiography. Shortly after the April 1978 coup, the *Kabul Times* began a series of articles on Afghan history that was to run at least until the end of the year and was clearly designed to rewrite the historical record according to "correct" ideological precepts. Though Ghulam Nabi features prominently as a martyr to Nader Shah's bestiality (*Kabul Times*, June 21, 22, and 23, 1978; the prose is extravagantly lurid), parts of his background are strangely obscured: for example, his biography mentions an earlier diplomatic tour in Moscow in the early 1920s but nothing about his presence in the USSR in 1929, even though he was ambassador there at the time. There is no mention whatsoever of his march into northern Afghanistan, and no effort is made either to deny or to detail the subversive activities for which he was executed. It is almost as if a carefully sanitized dossier had been made available to the propagandist whose duty it was to write the articles.

48. Conversation with Mr. Hashmat Gobar, whose father, Mir Mohammed Gobar (Ghubar) had been a member of the Jawanan Afghan and was imprisoned by Nader Shah shortly before the latter's assassination.

49. Louis Dupree and Linette Albert, eds., *Afghanistan in the 1970s* (New York: Praeger, 1974), p. 30.

50. Ibid.

51. Ibid.

52. Louis Dupree, *Red Flag over the Hindu Kush—Part I: Leftist Movements in Afghanistan*, American Universities Field Staff Report (AUFS), Asia 1979, no. 44, September 1979, LD–2–79, p. 17.

Chapter 3

1. Louis Dupree, *Afghanistan* (Princeton, N.J.: Princeton University Press, 1973), p. 480.

2. Ibid., p. 481.

3. Vartan Gregorian, *The Emergence of Modern Afghanistan* (Stanford: Stanford University Press, 1969), pp. 389–91.

4. Peter Franck, *Afghanistan Between East and West* (Washington, D.C.: National Planning Association, 1960), p. 6.

5. Ibid., p. 37.

6. Ibid., pp. 36–45.

7. Dupree, *Afghanistan*, pp. 499–507; and Franck, *Between East and West*, p. 66.

8. Louis Dupree, *Afghanistan's "Big Gamble": Part II—The Economic and*

Strategic Aspects of Soviet Aid, American Universities Field Staff Report (AUFS), South Asia Series, vol. 4, no. 4, May 1960, LD–4–60, p. 6.

9. Dupree, *Afghanistan*, p. 492.
10. Ibid., p. 491.
11. Ibid., p. 512.
12. V. M. Vinogradov et al., eds., *Sovetsko-afganskiye otnosheniya, 1919–1969* (Moscow: Politizdat, 1971), p. 7.
13. Dupree, *Afghanistan*, p. 493.
14. Vinogradov et al., *Sovetsko-afganskiye otnosheniya*, pp. 110–12.
15. Dupree, *Afghanistan's "Big Gamble": Part II*, AUFS, LD–4–60, p. 7.
16. Ibid.
17. Franck, *Between East and West*, p. 9.
18. Y. Volkov et al., *The Truth About Afghanistan—Documents, Facts, Eyewitness Reports* (Moscow: Novosti Press Publishing House, 1980), p. 30.
19. Anthony Arnold, *Afghanistan's Two-Party Communism: Parcham and Khalq* (Stanford: Hoover Institution Press, 1983), p. 12; Henry S. Bradsher, *Afghanistan and the Soviet Union* (Durham, N.C.: Duke University Press, 1983), pp. 19–20; and Dupree, *Afghanistan*, pp. 510–11.

Chapter 4

1. Louis Dupree, *Afghanistan* (Princeton, N.J.: Princeton University Press, 1973), pp. 494–95.
2. Louis Dupree, *Afghanistan's Slow March to Democracy*, American Universities Field Staff Report (AUFS), South Asia Series, vol. 7, no. 1, January 1963, LD–1–63, p. 12.
3. Dupree, *Afghanistan*, p. 495.
4. Richard S. Newell, *The Politics of Afghanistan* (Ithaca, N.Y.: Cornell University Press, 1972), p. 66.
5. V. M. Vinogradov et al., eds., *Sovetsko-afganskiye otnosheniya, 1919–1969* (Moscow: Politizdat, 1971), pp. 113–14.
6. Peter Franck, *Afghanistan Between East and West* (Washington, D.C.: National Planning Association, 1960), p. 55.
7. Ibid. Interestingly, this agreement is not included in the compilation of Soviet-Afghan agreements listed in Vinogradov et al., *Sovetsko-afganskiye otnosheniya*.
8. Dupree, *Afghanistan*, p. 513.
9. Franck, *Between East and West*, p. 56.

10. Ibid., pp. 12–13.

11. Anthony Arnold, *Afghanistan's Two-Party Communism: Parcham and Khalq* (Stanford: Hoover Institution Press, 1983), p. 12.

12. W. Fraser-Tytler, *Afghanistan* (London: Oxford University Press, 1967), p. 321.

13. Louis Dupree, *Afghanistan's "Big Gamble": Part II—The Economic and Strategic Aspects of Soviet Aid*, American Universities Field Staff Report (AUFS), South Asia Series, vol. 4, no. 4, May 1960, LD–4–60, p. 7.

14. Franck, *Between East and West*, p. 12.

15. Dupree, *Afghanistan*, p. 507. Dupree's figure of 3600 miles for this road seems excessive.

16. Franck, *Between East and West*, p. 12.

17. Vinogradov et al., *Sovetsko-afganskiye otnosheniya*, pp. 115–17.

18. Dupree, *Aghanistan*, p. 508.

19. Ibid., p. 499.

20. Louis Dupree and Linette Albert, eds. *Afghanistan in the 1970s* (New York: Praeger, 1974), p. 43.

21. Vinogradov et al., *Sovetsko-afganskiye otnosheniya*, pp. 122–25.

22. Ibid., pp. 125–27.

23. Dupree, *Afghanistan*, p. 518.

24. Ibid., p. 508.

25. Franck, *Between East and West*, p. 57.

26. Vinogradov et al., *Sovetsko-afganskiye otnosheniya*, pp. 129–34.

27. Louis Dupree, *American Private Enterprise in Afghanistan: The Investment Climate, Particularly as It Relates to One Company*, American Universities Field Staff Report (AUFS), South Asia Series, vol. 4, no. 9, December 1960, LD–9–60, p. 4.

28. Franck, *Between East and West*, p. 461.

29. Vinogradov et al., *Sovetsko-afganskiye otnosheniya*, pp. 127–29.

30. Dupree, *Afghanistan*, pp. 514–22.

31. Franck, *Between East and West*, pp. 45–46.

32. Ibid., p. 72 (quoting *Mutual Security Act of 1958*, Hearings, vol. 2, p. 1707).

33. Ibid., p. 67; Newell, *Politics of Afghanistan*, pp. 128–29.

34. Franck, Newell, Dupree et al. reached this conclusion.

35. Dupree, *Afghanistan's "Big Gamble": Part II*, AUFS, LD–4–60, p. 3.

36. Vinogradov et al., *Sovetsko-afganskiye otnosheniya*, pp. 185–86.

37. Franck, *Between East and West*, p. 65.

38. Vinogradov et al., *Sovetsko-afganskiye otnosheniya*, p. 156.
39. Ibid., pp. 179–82.
40. Personal conversations with the author by both engineers and attachés.
41. Dupree, *Afghanistan*, p. 511.
42. Louis Dupree, *The Mountains Go to Mohammed Zahir: Observations on Afghanistan's Reactions to Visits by Nixon, Bulganin-Khrushchev, Eisenhower, and Khrushchev*, American Universities Field Staff Report (AUFS), South Asia Series, vol. 4, no. 6, May 1960, LD–6–60, p. 25.
43. Franck, *Between East and West*, p. 12.
44. Fraser-Tytler, *Afghanistan*, p. 322.
45. Ibid., p. 323.
46. Dupree, *Afghanistan*, p. 539.
47. Ibid., pp. 544–45.
48. Louis Dupree, *"Pushtunistan": The Problem and Its Larger Implications*, American Universities Field Staff Report (AUFS), South Asia Series, vol. 5, no. 1, October 1961, LD–1–61, p. 11.
49. Dupree, *Afghanistan*, p. 541.
50. Dupree, *"Pushtunistan,"* AUFS, LD–1–61, p. 10.
51. Fraser-Tytler, *Afghanistan*, p. 326.
52. Louis Dupree, *The Decade of Daoud Ends: Implications of Afghanistan's Change of Government*, American Universities Field Staff Report (AUFS), South Asia Series, vol. 7, no. 7, May 1963, LD–7–63, p. 3.
53. Ibid., p. 6.
54. Ibid., p. 11.

Chapter 5

1. Louis Dupree and Linette Albert, eds., *Afghanistan in the 1970s* (New York: Praeger, 1974), p. 54. The simile is from a former cabinet minister.
2. Louis Dupree, *An Informal Talk with King Mohammed Zahir of Afghanistan*, American Field Staff Report (AUFS), South Asia Series, vol. 7, no. 9, July 1963, LD–9–63, p. 3.
3. Louis Dupree, *Constitutional Development and Cultural Change—Part III: The 1964 Afghan Constitution (Articles 1–56)*, American Field Staff Report (AUFS), South Asia Series, vol. 9, no. 3, September 1965, LD–3–65, p. 17.
4. Louis Dupree, *Afghanistan* (Princeton: Princeton University Press, 1973), p. 590.

5. G. L. Grassmuck, L. W. Adamec, and F. H. Irwin, eds., *Afghanistan: Some New Approaches* (Ann Arbor: University of Michigan Press, 1969), p. 171.

6. For the information in this and the succeeding two paragraphs I am indebted to Mr. Hashmat Gobar, whose late father, Mir Mohammed Gobar (Ghubar), played an important role in the political ferment of the time. In the first edition of this book I relayed mistaken information that implicated him in the Nader Shah assassination. In fact, Gobar had been jailed by Nader Shah several months before the fatal shots were fired.

7. Anthony Arnold, *Afghanistan's Two-Party Communism: Parcham and Khalq* (Stanford: Hoover Institution Press, 1983), p. 6.

8. Dupree, *Afghanistan*, p. 497.

9. Louis Dupree, *Red Flag over the Hindu Kush—Part I: Leftist Movements in Afghanistan*, American Universities Field Staff Report (AUFS), Asia 1979, no. 44, September 1979, LD–2–79, p. 6.

10. Peter Franck, *Afghanistan Between East and West* (Washington, D.C.: National Planning Association, 1960), pp. 10, 72.

11. "The Revolution in Afghanistan," *The New Left Review*, no. 112 (November–December 1978), p. 22.

12. Ibid.

13. Dupree, *Afghanistan*, pp. 591–92.

14. Ibid., p. 649.

15. R. T. Akhramovich, *Outline History of Afghanistan After the Second World War* (Moscow: Izdatel'stvo vostochnoy literatury, 1966), p. 183.

16. R. T. Akhramovich, *Afganistan v 1961–66 gg.* (Moscow: Nauka, 1967), p. 183.

17. Grassmuck et al., *Afghanistan: Some New Approaches*, pp. 184–85.

18. Dupree, *Afghanistan*, pp. 596–97.

19. Louis Dupree, *Afghanistan: 1966*, American Universities Field Staff Report (AUFS), South Asia Series, vol. 10, no. 4, July 1966, LD–4–66, p. 12.

20. Ibid.

21. Dupree, *Afghanistan*, pp. 602–3.

22. Arnold, *Afghanistan's Two-Party Communism*, pp. 34–36.

23. Dupree, *Afghanistan: 1966*, AUFS, LD–4–66, p. 13.

24. Dupree and Albert, *Afghanistan in the 1970s*, p. 62.

25. Dupree, *Red Flag—Part I*, AUFS, LD–2–79, pp. 7, 9.

26. *Kabul Times*, July 5, 1978.

27. Richard S. Newell, *The Politics of Afghanistan* (Ithaca, N.Y.: Cornell University Press, 1972), p. 144.

Chapter 6

1. Louis Dupree, *A Note on Afghanistan: 1974*, American Universities Field Staff Report (AUFS), South Asia Series, vol. 18, no. 8 (Afghanistan), September 1974, LD–4–74, p. 1.

2. Louis Dupree, *Red Flag over the Hindu Kush—Part I: Leftist Movements in Afghanistan*, American Universities Field Staff Report (AUFS), Asia 1979, no. 44, September 1979, LD–2–79, p. 7.

3. *Kabul New Times*, May 8, 1980.

4. Dupree, *Afghanistan: 1974*, AUFS, LD–4–74, p. 19.

5. Dupree, *Red Flag—Part I*, AUFS, LD–2–79, p. 12.

6. Dupree, *Afghanistan: 1974*, AUFS, LD–4–74, p. 2.

7. Louis Dupree, *Afghanistan* (Princeton: Princeton University Press, 1973), pp. 757–58.

8. Ibid.

9. Dupree, *Red Flag—Part I*, AUFS, LD–2–79, p. 9.

10. Ibid., p. 10.

11. Louis Dupree, *Toward Representative Government in Afghanistan—Part I: The First Five Steps*, American Universities Field Staff Report (AUFS), Asia 1978, no. 1, February 1978, LD–1–78, p. 10.

12. Dupree, *Red Flag—Part I*, AUFS, LD–2–79, p. 10. In an earlier description of this event, Dupree hinted that Maiwandwal might have been murdered and that he was anathema to leftists; in the work cited here, the murder allegation is explicit, and though Dupree's term for the unidentified murderers ("extreme leftists") remains undefined in this case, the widespread Parcham penetration of the Ministry of Interior (under whose aegis Maiwandwal was being held) provides circumstantial evidence that Parcham was responsible.

13. Dupree, *Toward Representative Government*, AUFS, LD–1–78, p. 1.

14. Dupree, *Afghanistan: 1974*, AUFS, LD–4–74, p. 19.

15. Dupree, *Red Flag—Part I*, AUFS, LD–2–79, p. 12. Dupree lists Abdulellah along with Hassan Sharq as someone with close connections to Parcham but probably not a member. Whatever his ideological bent, Abdulellah was not widely respected in the Daoud cabinet; his appointment was commonly ascribed to family loyalty, his father having been a close friend and confidant of the man who raised Daoud and Naim after their father's assassination.

16. Conversations in 1980 with a former ranking U.S. embassy official. Several ranking Afghans had told him privately of Jalalar's undeclared pro-Soviet orientation.

17. Dupree, *Red Flag—Part I*, AUFS, LD–2–79, p. 13.

18. Ibid. Dupree (without citing his sources) states that these individuals were all recruited into Khalq by Taraki [*sic*] only in 1977. Inasmuch as all three vanished under the Khalq regime of Hafizullah Amin in 1979 and emerged as ministers only after Soviet forces returned the Parchami Babrak to power, it seems likely that their primary allegiance was to Parcham, if not (as seems most likely of all) directly to the USSR. If this is the case, one must also question the year 1977 as the date of their recruitment to a pro-Soviet cause; it probably occurred earlier, most likely during their training in the USSR.

19. Dupree, *Toward Representative Government*, AUFS, LD–1–78, pp. 7–9.

20. Dupree, *Afghanistan: 1974*, AUFS, LD–4–74, p. 9.

21. Louis Dupree, *Red Flag over the Hindu Kush—Part II: The Accidental Coup, or Taraki in Blunderland*, American Universities Field Staff Report (AUFS), Asia 1979, no. 45, September 1979, LD–3–79, p. 1.

22. Louis Dupree, *Afghanistan 1977: Does Trade Plus Aid Guarantee Development?* American Universities Field Staff Report (AUFS), South Asia Series, vol. 21, no. 3, August 1977, LD–3–77, p. 4.

23. Louis Dupree, *Toward Representative Government in Afghanistan— Part III: Steps Six Through Nine—and Beyond?* American Universities Field Staff Report (AUFS), Asia 1978, no. 14, February 1978, LD–2–78, pp. 1–3.

24. Private conversation with a member of Daoud's extended family in 1979. The source had heard this directly from Naim on the latter's return from Moscow. Naim was concerned that Daoud did not seem to sense the depth of Soviet ire that he (Naim) had detected.

25. Dupree, *Red Flag—Part I*, AUFS, LD–2–79, p. 11.

26. Dupree, *Red Flag—Part II*, AUFS, LD–3–79. p. 1.

27. Ibid., p. 4.

28. Anthony Arnold, *Afghanistan's Two-Party Communism: Parcham and Khalq* (Stanford: Hoover Institution Press, 1983), pp. 57–58.

Chapter 7

1. *International Herald Tribune*, May 2, 1978.

2. *On the Saur Revolution* (Kabul: The Political Department of the People's

Democratic Party of Afghanistan in the Armed Forces of Afghanistan, May 22, 1978), p. 11.

3. Ibid., p. 12.

4. Ibid., p. 21.

5. Ibid., p. 4.

6. Anthony Arnold, *Afghanistan's Two-Party Communism: Parcham and Khalq* (Stanford: Hoover Institution Press, 1983), p. 59. See also Louis Dupree, *Red Flag over the Hindu Kush—Part II: The Accidental Coup, or Taraki in Blunderland*, American Universities Field Staff Report (AUFS), Asia 1979, no. 45, September 1979, LD–3–79, p. 6.

7. *Daily Telegraph*, May 4, 1978; *Financial Times*, May 4, 1978.

8. *Daily Telegraph*, May 4, 1978.

9. *Kabul Times*, May 3, 1978.

10. *On the Saur Revolution*, p. 12.

11. Dupree, *Red Flag—Part II*, AUFS, LD–3–79, p. 5.

12. Ibid.

13. *On the Saur Revolution*, p. 14.

14. Ibid., pp. 17–19.

15. Ibid., p. 28.

16. Dupree, *Red Flag—Part II*, AUFS, LD–3–79, p. 14.

17. *International Herald Tribune*, February 24–25, 1978.

18. Ibid., May 2, 1978.

19. Ibid., May 5, 1978.

20. *Guardian*, May 8, 1978.

21. Dupree, *Red Flag—Part II*, AUFS, LD–3–79, p. 13. Amin was later to raise this figure to 101.

22. Personal conversation with a former prisoner who had talked with Republican Guard prisoners before their execution.

23. *Kabul Times*, November 28, 1978.

24. Dupree, *Red Flag—Part II*, AUFS, LD–3–79, p. 14 and *Red Flag over the Hindu Kush—Part I: Leftist Movements in Afghanistan*, American Universities Field Staff Report (AUFS), Asia 1979, no. 44, September 1979, LD–2–79, p. 13. Dupree avers that in 1973 Qader was a "non-leftist coup participant." If so, he became a convert not too long thereafter. It is more probable that he came under Soviet influence earlier, during training in the USSR.

25. *On the Saur Revolution*, p. 29.

26. *Kabul Times*, August 6, 1978.

27. *Daily Telegraph*, August 18, 1979.

28. *Kabul Times*, September 23, 1978. There were eight pages instead of the usual four in this issue.

29. Ibid.

30. Ibid.

31. Ibid., May 6, May 7, and May 15, 1978, for example.

32. Selig S. Harrison, "Nightmare in Baluchistan," *Foreign Policy*, no. 32, Fall 1978, pp. 136–59.

33. See "Afghan Tribesmen in Revolt," *Daily Telegraph*, June 5, 1978, for an early description of the process of disaffection in the countryside.

34. *Kabul Times*, September 24 and September 25, 1978, for example; many other examples were to follow.

35. Ibid., November 26, 1978.

36. Ibid., October 26, 1978.

37. *Kabul Times*, December 9, 1978. This article was later used to justify the Soviet invasion.

38. *Economist*, January 13, 1979.

39. Arnold, *Afghanistan's Two-Party Communism*, pp. 82–83; Henry S. Bradsher, *Afghanistan and the Soviet Union* (Durham, N.C.: Duke University Press, 1983), pp. 98–100; Y. Volkov et al., *The Truth About Afghanistan: Documents, Facts, Eyewitness Reports* (Moscow: Novosti Press Agency Publishing House, 1980), p. 42; and U.S. Department of State, *The Kidnapping and Death of Ambassador Adolph Dubs, February 14, 1979*, undated but written in late 1979. Investigation of the Dubs murder should be reopened. The allegation that an obscure breakaway Marxist faction called *Settam-e-Melli* was responsible is dubious at best. (Bradsher gives this solution, but his cited source for it, *The Kidnapping and Death of Ambassador Adolph Dubs* contains no mention whatsoever of *Settam-e-Melli*. In spite of the time that has elapsed and the subsequent violent deaths of all major Afghan officials who figured in the case, we are probably in a better position now to analyze the tragedy than we were in 1979–80. Today terrorism is better understood, and among the flood of defectors and refugees that have poured over the Afghan border into Pakistan since the Soviet invasion there may well be knowledgeable witnesses. One such, a former Kabul policeman, for example, has already claimed that at least one of the kidnappers was an identified member of the PDPA Parcham faction (François Missen, *Le Syndrome de Kaboul* [Aix-en-Provence: Edisud, 1980], p. 168). If true, this has momentous implications in view of the close KGB association with Parcham. A careful canvassing of other potential sources should be undertaken to confirm or deny this information and to uncover other clues.

40. *International Herald Tribune*, April 14–15, 1979.

41. *Daily Telegraph*, March 29, 1979.

42. *International Herald Tribune*, March 29, 1979.

43. Ibid., April 14–15, 1979.

44. *Christian Science Monitor*, February 4, 1980.

45. *International Herald Tribune*, August 7, 1979.

46. Ibid., August 13, 1979.

47. Patrick J. Garrity, "The Soviet Military Stake in Afghanistan, 1956–79," *RUSI: Journal of the Royal United Services Institute for Defence Studies* 125, no. 3 (September 1980): 35.

48. Astrid von Borcke, "Die Intervention in Afghanistan: Das Ende der sowjetischen Koexistenzpolitik?" *Berichte des Bundesinstituts fuer ostwissenschaftliche und internationale Studien*, no. 6 (1980), p. 4.

49. *Economist*, January 5, 1980.

50. *Guardian*, October 29, 1979.

51. *Economist*, November 3, 1979.

52. *New York Times*, September 20, 1979. Two weeks earlier, a *New York Times* article credited to "Western and Asian diplomatic sources" in Kabul warned with impeccable logic that the USSR was moving toward "direct, broad military intervention." This one-of-a-kind prediction (which is not known to have been echoed in any official U.S. traffic or other media outlets) may possibly have been a cleverly placed Soviet trial balloon to elicit possible Western responses to a Soviet invasion. If so, it appears no one was listening; when the invasion did come, it shocked everyone. (*New York Times*, September 6, 1979, p. 2; and Arnold, *Afghanistan's Two-Party Communism*, pp. 89–90.)

53. *Kabul Times*, September 16, 1979.

54. Ibid., September 12, 1979.

55. *Economist*, November 3, 1979.

56. Ibid.

57. *Kabul Times*, September 15, 1979.

58. Ibid., September 18, 1979.

59. Ibid., September 17, 1979.

60. Ibid., September 19, 1979.

Chapter 8

1. *Kabul New Times*, January 27 and 28, 1980. This paper is the replacement for the *Kabul Times*, which ceased publication with the Soviet invasion.

2. *New York Times*, September 19, 1979.

3. *Kabul Times*, September 20, 22, 24, and 30, 1979.

4. Ibid., September 24, and October 6 and 7, 1979.

5. Patrick J. Garrity, "The Soviet Military Stake in Afghanistan, 1956–79," *RUSI: Journal of the Royal United Services Institute for Defence Studies* 125, no. 3 (September 1980): 35. The stay of the delegation in Afghanistan lasted for nearly two months according to this source, indicating that it would have departed in early October.

6. *Kabul Times*, November 25, 1979.

7. Ibid., October 29, 1979.

8. Ibid., October 3, 1979, for example.

9. Ibid., October 11, 1979.

10. Ibid., October 2, 1979.

11. Ibid., November 17 and 21, 1979.

12. Ibid., November 6, 1979.

13. Ibid., November 7 and 8, 1979.

14. Ibid., November 22, 1979.

15. Ibid., December 6, 1979.

16. Ibid., September 16, 1979.

17. Ibid., October 8 and 15, 1979, respectively.

18. Ibid., November 17, 18, and 26, 1979, respectively.

19. Ibid., November 25, 1979.

20. Ibid., November 18, 1979.

21. Ibid., October 25, and November 5, 13, and 21, 1979.

22. *New York Times*, October 17, 1979; and Dupree, *Afghanistan* (Princeton, N.J.: Princeton University Press, 1973), p. 612.

23. *New York Times*, October 16, 1979.

24. Conversation with Dr. Sarwar Nassery, former Afghan Foreign Office official, in early November 1980.

25. Henry S. Bradsher, *Afghanistan and the Soviet Union* (Durham, N.C.: Duke University Press, 1983), pp. 96–97; and *Daily Telegraph*, June 2, 1979.

26. Anthony Arnold, *Afghanistan's Two-Party Communism: Parcham and Khalq* (Stanford: Hoover Institution Press, 1983), pp. 132–33.

27. Patrick J. Garrity, "The Soviet Military Stake in Afghanistan, 1956–79," *Journal of the Royal United Services Institute for Defence Studies* 125, no. 3 (September 1980): 35–36.

28. Ibid.

29. Ibid.

30. *Kabul Times*, December 1, 1979.

31. Ibid., December 16, 1979.

32. *Foreign Report*, no. 1614 (January 9, 1980), pp. 1–2.

33. *Washington Post*, February 18, 1980. This story first appeared in the *London Observer* on February 17. It has all the earmarks of a Soviet disinformation piece. Some years later a version citing as its source Roy Medvedev, the Soviet semidissident historian, alleged that Amin was supposed to have been replaced peaceably by Babrak some 2–3 days after the Soviet army had secured Kabul, but due to "unanticipated developments" in connection with the Soviet army takeover, Amin met a premature and unforeseen death (*Le Monde diplomatique*, September 1983: 13).

34. *Economist*, June 14, 1980. Bradsher (pp. 175–78) offers the intriguing theory that the wounding of Assadullah took place during an assassination attempt against Hafizullah Amin himself, arranged by Paputin and/or an unidentified, ranking KGB general, also allegedly visiting Kabul at the time. He believes Amin's death warrant was issued at a November 26 CPSU Politburo meeting, and that the intention was to replace Amin with another PDPA figure who would then issue the necessary invitation for intervention. From available evidence, including the timing of the Paputin visit, it seems more likely to me that any such authorization would have been considered as a final fallback measure, to be employed only in the event that Amin himself could not be persuaded to sanction the invasion.

35. "The Soviet Military Stake," *Journal of Royal United Services Institute for Defence Studies*, September 1980, p. 36.

36. Ibid.

37. *Kabul Times*, December 22, 1979.

38. *San Francisco Chronicle*, December 22, 1979.

39. Edward N. Luttwak, "After Afghanistan, What?" *Commentary* 69, no. 4 (April 1980): 47.

40. Personal conversations with an Afghan émigré in January 1980.

41. *Kabul Times*, December 25, 1979.

42. *Le Soir* (Brussels), February 12, 1980.

43. "Afghanistan—Soviet Occupation," *Background Brief* (London: United Kingdom Foreign and Commonwealth Office), February 1980.

44. A. G. Noorani, "Afghanistan and the Rule of Law," *The Review* (New York: American Association for the International Commission of Jurists, June 1980), p. 43.

45. James Phillips, "The Soviet Invasion of Afghanistan," *Backgrounder* (Washington, D.C.: Heritage Foundation, January 9, 1980), p. 3.

Chapter 9

1. Pierce G. Fredericks, *The Sepoy and the Cossack* (New York: World Publishing, 1971), p. 199.

2. John F. Baddeley, *The Russian Conquest of the Caucasus* (London: Longmans, Green and Co., 1908), pp. xxxvii–xxxviii.

3. M. Jean Jose Puig puts it with succinct elegance: "Mais s'il est relativement facile—du moins en Afghanistan—d'occuper le lieu du pouvoir, il est autrement difficile d'exercer le pouvoir" (*Esprit*, April 1982, p. 76).

4. *Christian Science Monitor*, May 31, 1984, p. 1.

5. *London Times*, May 30, 1984, p. 5; *Afghanistan Forum* 12, no. 3 (June 1984): 5; and *Economist*, January 8, 1983, p. 36.

6. *Afghanistan Forum* 12, no. 2 (March 1984): 7.

7. *Afghanistan Forum Newsletter* 11, no. 4 (October 1983): 16; and *New York Times*, June 6, 1984, p. 7, May 27, 1984, p. 6, and April 25, 1984, p. 1; and Henry S. Bradsher, *Afghanistan and the Soviet Union* (Durham, N.C.: Duke University Press, 1983), pp. 210–11.

8. Baddeley, *The Russian Conquest of the Caucasus*, pp. 130–32; and Anthony Arnold, *Afghanistan's Two-Party Communism: Parcham and Khalq* (Stanford: Hoover Institution Press, 1983), pp. 128–29.

9. *Afghanistan Forum* 12, no. 3 (June 1984): 4. The statistics were included in a *Pakistan Times* article, which in turn drew on the *Swiss Press Review* and an article by Tad Szulc (original publication not cited). Although too precise to be fully credible, the Szulc figures on losses of matériel are somewhat lower than those reported from other sources. His estimate of personnel losses are also at the low end of those reported elsewhere.

10. Ibid., pp. 3, 4; and *Economist*, January 8, 1983, p. 36. DRA figures for the cost of the war were in the *Kabul New Times* of July 7, 1983; and in *Foreign Broadcast Information Service (FBIS)* 8, March 6, 1984, p. C-1.

11. *London Times*, June 2, 1984, p. 2; and *Afghanistan Forum* 12, no. 3 (June 1984): 4.

12. The only specific charge that has not been supported is the overt inclusion of *Settam-e-Melli* as part of a government of national reconciliation. The implication of that group in the murder of Ambassador Dubs may have led the USSR and PDPA to shy away from acknowledging *Settam-e-Melli* support, though there have been persistent rumors that persons in the group enjoy full Soviet confidence and in late 1982 were being groomed

for a political role in Badakhshan (*Afghanistan Realities*, no. 9 [January–February 1983]:ˑ20).

13. Arnold, *Afghanistan's Two-Party Communism*, pp. 116–21; and *Kabul New Times*, July 7, 1983, and November 8, 1984.

14. Arnold, *Afghanistan's Two-Party Communism*, pp. 124–25.

15. *International Affairs* (Moscow), no. 5 (1983): 42.

16. *Kabul New Times*, July 7, 1983, and May 5, 1984; *Economist*, January 8, 1983, p. 36; and Richard F. Staar, ed., *Yearbook on International Communist Affairs* (Stanford: Hoover Institution Press, 1984), p. 187.

17. Ibid., June 26 and July 7, 1983, and April 14, 1984.

18. Ibid., July 7, 1983; and *Afghanistan Newsletter* 10, no. 4 (October 1982): 5.

19. *Kabul New Times*, July 7, 1983.

20. Arnold, *Afghanistan's Two-Party Communism*, p. 118; and *Kabul New Times*, April 24 and July 7, 1983, and May 5, 1984.

21. *Kabul New Times*, April 24, 1983; May 5, 1984.

22. *Afghanistan Newsletter* 10, no. 4 (October 1983): 5.

23. *Kabul New Times*, July 7, 1983.

24. Ibid., April 14 and May 5, 1984.

25. *New York Times*, September 7, 1983, p. I-4.

26. Arnold, *Afghanistan's Two-Party Communism*, pp. 121–23. The anti-Khalqi coup plot by the Parchamis in summer 1978 included formation of a "United National Front" for this purpose. Babrak suggested that same title in his first speech following the Soviet invasion, but later modified it to the present name. Despite continuous propaganda in its favor, the organization took another eighteen months to form.

27. *Le Monde diplomatique* 354 (September 1983): 17; and *Kabul New Times*, April 25, 1984. The lower figure in the latter source appears not to have been merely the accidental dropping of a digit but probably reflects inadvertent release of normally restricted statistics. The same article, entitled "Facts and Figures," gave a membership for the Democratic Organization of Afghan Women (DOAW) of 19,287, well under half the 50,000 members claimed for DOAW by Dr. Najibullah two years before (*FBIS*, 8, April 30, 1982, p. C-1).

28. Arnold, *Afghanistan's Two-Party Communism*, p. 122; and *New York Times*, July 17, 1981, p. 5.

29. *Kabul New Times*, May 26, 1984; and *Le Monde diplomatique* 354 (September 1983): 17–18.

30. *Kabul New Times*, June 19, 1983. Russianisms in the English-language

Kabul New Times formerly occurred often, but seem to have vanished in 1984. Their place was taken by an occasional lapse into Central European distortions, e.g., "He with local accent spoke frankly . . . A brief smile separated his lips from each other, and he lifted with his hand his cap a bittle upper his forehead" (*Kabul New Times*, March 29, 1984).

31. *Kabul New Times*, May 31, June 8, June 22, and June 23, 1983. He appeared in other issues as well.

32. *Kabul New Times*, September 22, 1982, and April 24, 1983; and Staar, ed., *Yearbook on International Communist Affairs*, p. 189.

33. Ibid., June 23 and June 25, 1983.

34. Ibid., December 15, May 22, and June 6, 1983.

35. *Afghanistan Forum Newsletter* 11, no. 4 (October 1983): 24–25, 37.

36. Ibid., 46; *Afghanistan Forum Newsletter* 12, no. 1 (January 1984): 38; *Afghanistan Forum* 12, no. 3 (June 1984): 3.

37. *Kabul New Times*, October 31, 1983, and January 28, April 16, 17, and 23, 1984; Bradsher, *Afghanistan and the Soviet Union*, p. 229; *Afghanistan Forum Newsletter* 11, no. 2 (March 1983): 40, 12, no. 1 (January 1984): 10; and *Afghanistan Forum* 12, no. 3 (June 1984): 4, 20.

38. *Kabul New Times*, August 14, 1982.

39. Ibid., April 25, 1984; *Afghanistan Forum Newsletter* 11, no. 4 (October 1983): 35; and *Afghanistan Forum* 12, no. 3 (June 1984): 33.

40. *New York Times*, August 20, 1981, p. 3.

41. *Kabul New Times*, May 24, 1983; and *Afghanistan Forum Newsletter* 11, no. 2 (March 1983): 12.

42. *Kabul New Times*, April 5 and 23, 1983; and *Afghanistan Council Newsletter* 11, no. 4 (October 1983): 4, 23.

43. *Kabul New Times*, April 12, 1983, and March 14 and April 2, 1984.

44. *Afghanistan Forum Newsletter* 11, no. 2 (March 1983): 27, and no. 4 (October 1983): 21–23.

Chapter 10

1. W. Fraser-Tytler, *Afghanistan* (London: Oxford University Press, 1967), p. 336.

2. *Pravda*, January 13, 1980, p. 1.

3. Henry S. Bradsher, *Afghanistan and the Soviet Union* (Durham, N.C.: Duke University Press, 1983), pp. 127–29. Bradsher's analysis of the Soviet perception of the "correlation of forces" is a sobering one.

4. *New York Times*, April 25, 1981, p. 1. The United States also imposed

other economic sanctions, from curtailment of Soviet fishing privileges in American waters to restrictions on trade, but none had as much impact as the grain embargo.

5. It is interesting that the USSR insisted on taking its eventual revenge in kind, by boycotting the 1984 Los Angeles summer Olympics. This devotion to reciprocity if anything detracted still further from its prestige and lost it a chance to prove its sports superiority. In choosing a self-defeating sanction the USSR helped offset an equally ill-considered U.S. "punishment" for the invasion, the 1980 cancellation of a Soviet-American consular agreement that sacrificed an existing U.S. outpost in Kiev for a potential Soviet consulate in New York—where, courtesy of the UN, a large Soviet presence was already on hand.

6. *Christian Science Monitor*, May 23, 1980, p. 5.

7. *San Francisco Chronicle*, March 11, 1983, p. 22.

8. *Washington Post*, October 22, 1983, p. 1. The number of refugees is regularly exaggerated (to about 4 million as of mid-1984), a custom found profitable by the Pakistani government in soliciting international help for the refugees, by individual Afghan heads of household who receive more rations if their families have one or two fictional members, and by members of the working press who rarely reject a higher number of almost anything. The author's personal assessment, admittedly based largely on the automatic discounting of statistics originating in that part of the world, is a total exodus of 2.5–3.0 million, an impressive tide of human misery even at this reduced level.

9. *Economist*, January 8, 1983, p. 35.

10. *Afghanistan Council Newsletter* 10, no. 1 (January 1982): 23–24. This is a reprint of an article by Carl Bernstein that first appeared in *The New Republic* in July 1981. See also *Time Magazine*, June 11, 1984: 38–40.

11. *New York Times*, May 4, 1983, p. 1; and *Wall Street Journal*, April 9, 1984, p. 34.

12. *Wall Street Journal*, March 17, 1983, p. 30.

13. *New York Times*, June 12, 1983, p. 7, June 16, 1983, p. 6, and June 22, 1984, p. 5.

14. *Afghanistan Forum Newsletter* 11, no. 2 (March 1983): 12; and *Kabul New Times*, June 7 and December 25, 1983, and January 25, 1984. The Afghan statistics are contradictory. They claim that the Soviets gave $300 million credit for 2.4 billion cubic meters of gas at a price "equal to the West European gas market." Such payment for that volume of gas actually would imply nearly ten times the going free-market price in 1983–84. Had the Soviets been so generous, Afghan propaganda would scarcely have claimed mere equality. Even with a production of 5.0 billion cubic

meters, the price would have been far above normal. Somewhere, it seems, a digit has been misplaced.

15. *Afghanistan Forum Newsletter* 11, no. 2 (March 1983): 12.

16. Ibid., p. 17.

17. *Kabul New Times*, October 23 and October 27, 1983. Barter trade was to account for $800 million of this trade, a 15 percent increase over 1983.

18. *Afghanistan Forum Newsletter* 11, no. 2 (March 1983): 12. The other countries were Vietnam, Mongolia, and Cuba.

19. Ibid.

20. *Kabul New Times*, November 11, 1983. A similar situation of cross-border trade with Soviet frontier republics appears to have developed recently in Poland as well. It may or may not be significant that these two countries are the most rebellious in the Soviet family of nations.

21. The author once took to task a member of the Swedish Foreign Office for his country's smug condemnations of U.S. foreign policy in areas where Sweden had no interests, yet reluctance to criticize the USSR for its persecution of national minorities in the Baltic states, close at hand. "Yes," he replied genially, "because you are our good friends and will listen; it does no good to criticize the USSR."

22. Ladislav Bittman, *The Deception Game* (New York: Ballantine Books, 1972). This book should be required reading for editors, scholars, and anyone else responsible for assessing the reliability of information.

23. The sentencing of Pierre Charles Pathé, French editor of the KGB-sponsored but ostensibly noncommunist periodical *Synthese*, to five years in prison in May 1980 is a case in point. It is noteworthy that Pathé almost surely would not have been prosecuted for his agent-of-influence role (which probably was not technically illegal) if he had not combined it simultaneously with a more active spying career.

24. Anthony Arnold, *Afghanistan's Two-Party Communism: Parcham and Khalq* (Stanford: Hoover Institution Press, 1983), pp. 60–63.

25. *New York Times*, February 10, 1981, p. 23.

26. *Afghanistan Forum* 12, no. 2 (March 1984): 9; and *Le Monde diplomatique* 354 (September 1983): 13. For a brief analysis of Soviet Pavlovian diplomacy, see *Christian Science Monitor*, December 10, 1982, p. 22.

27. *Le Monde diplomatique* 354 (September 1983): 14; and Selig S. Harrison, "Nightmare in Baluchistan," *Foreign Policy*, no. 32 (Fall 1978): 136–59.

28. Arnold, *Afghanistan's Two-Party Communism*, p. 77. See also Amaury de Riencourt, "Pakistan and India in the Shadow of Afghanistan," *Foreign Affairs* (Winter 1982–83): pp. 416–37.

29. *The Manchester Guardian Weekly*, May 27, 1984, pp. 17–18; *Le Monde*

diplomatique 354 (September 1983): 16; *New York Times*, July 3, 1983, sect. 4, p. 12 (letter by Konrad Ege), and May 27, 1984, p. 6.

30. *New York Times*, November 6, 1980, p. 5; and *Christian Science Monitor*, June 4, 1980, p. 1.

31. Aleksander Smolar, "Afghanistan et Pologne," *Esprit* (January 1981): 91–95.

32. *New York Times*, June 24, 1981, p. 8. The Italian party's Giancarlo Pajetta was denied permission to speak about Afghanistan at the Twenty-sixth CPSU Congress in Moscow in March 1981 (*New York Times*, March 1, 1981, p. 3).

33. *Possev* 40, no. 6 (June 1984): 28; *London Times*, May 16, 1984, p. 10, and May 18, 1984, p. 11.

34. *Possev* 40, no. 6 (June 1984): 17; and *Christian Science Monitor*, August 10, 1984, p. 10. In its wars against Persia in the nineteenth century, Russia suffered so many defections that a battalion of Russian troops was formed to fight for the shah. The Vlasov movement, however, was far more massive and included nine out of the fifty Soviet generals captured by the Wehrmacht. Hitler's refusal (on racial grounds) to grant the movement the status of allies until the war was hopelessly lost was a key factor in his defeat on the eastern front.

35. *Washington Post*, May 27, 1983, p. A24.

36. Ronald R. Pope, "Afghanistan and the Influence of Public Opinion on Soviet Foreign Policy," *Asian Affairs*, July–August 1981: 346–52. R. V. Burks, "Die nahende Kriese in der Sowjetunion," *Osteuropa* 33, no. 6 (June 1983): 449–62, no. 7 (July 1983): 555–68, and no. 9 (September 1983): 705–23. These articles concern the possible collapse of the Soviet regime under its myriad problems.

Chapter 11

1. *Encounter* 57, no. 7 (July 1981): 90.

2. Henry S. Bradsher, *Afghanistan and the Soviet Union* (Durham, N.C.: Duke University Press), p. 175. Some have alleged that the USSR marched on Afghanistan because it was convinced the United States was about to invade Iran to liberate the hostages, and thus it expected to shuck off some of the blame for its own violent behavior on Washington. This seems most unlikely: the KGB keeps a keen and watchful eye on U.S. capabilities and intentions, and the Soviet leaders must have been aware that Washington had neither the muscle nor the stomach for a rescue attempt in 1979.

3. *Afghanistan Forum Newsletter* 10, no. 1 (January 1982): 23–24. In this reprint of a July 1981 article in *The New Republic*, Carl Bernstein states that before the invasion the United States provided the mujahideen with a small amount of covert aid in the form of medical supplies and communications equipment, but no arms.

4. Bradsher, *Afghanistan and the Soviet Union*, pp. 240–55.

5. Senate Concurrent Resolution No. 74; and House Concurrent Resolution No. 237. The Washington-based Federation for American Afghan Action (FAAA) and its associated American Afghan Education Fund lobbied in favor of this resolution and succeeded in attracting much legislative support, but the resolution remained stalled for reasons that were not entirely clear. It finally passed in November 1984 by a vote of 97–0 in the Senate and by a unanimous voice vote in the House of Representatives.

6. See *Afghanistan Council Newsletter* 10, no. 1 (January 1982): 23–24; and *Time*, July 11, 1984: 38–40 for the kinds of arms supplied. The FAAA has made bitter allegations that arms supplied by the United States have been dreadfully unreliable, inappropriate, and/or insufficient for the resistance's needs. It is impossible to substantiate or deny their accusations at this distance.

Selected Bibliography

Adamec, Ludwig W. *Afghanistan, 1900–23: A Diplomatic History*. Berkeley and Los Angeles: University of California Press, 1967.

———. *Afghanistan's Foreign Relations to the Mid-Twentieth Century: Relations with Russia, Germany, and Britain*. Tucson: University of Arizona Press, 1974.

———. *Who's Who of Afghanistan*. Graz, Austria: Akademische Druck- und Verlagsanstalt, 1975.

———. *Supplement to Who's Who of Afghanistan: The Democratic Republic of Afghanistan*. Graz, Austria: Akademische Druck- und Verlagsanstalt, 1979.

Afghan Realities. Paris: Afghan Information and Documentation Centre.

Afghanistan Council Newsletter. New York: Asia Society, 1968–82. (See also *Afghanistan Forum*, *Afghanistan Forum Newsletter*, and *Afghanistan Newsletter*. These publications provide probably the best compendium of media coverage of Afghanistan.) Produced approximately quarterly.

Afghanistan Forum. New York: Afghanistan Forum, 1984–.

Afghanistan Forum Newsletter. New York: Afghanistan Forum, 1983.

Afghanistan Newsletter. New York: Afghanistan Forum, October 1982.

Agabekov, Georges. *OGPU: The Russian Secret Terror*. Translated by W. Bunn. New York: Brentano's, 1931.

Akhramovich, Roman Timofeyevich. *Afganistan v 1961–66 gg* [Afghanistan, 1961–66]. Moscow: Nauka, 1967.

———. *Outline History of Afghanistan After the Second World War*. Moscow: Izdatel'stvo vostochnoy literatury, 1966.

————. *Sovetsko-afganskiye otnosheniya* [Soviet-Afghan relations]. Moscow: Politizdat, 1971.

Amin, Tahir. "Afghan Resistance: Past, Present, and Future." *Asian Survey*, April 1984: 373–99.

————. *Afghanistan Crisis*. Islamabad: Institute for Policy Studies, 1982.

Arnold, Anthony. *Afghanistan's Two-Party Communism: Parcham and Khalq*. Stanford: Hoover Institution Press, 1983.

Arunova, M. R.; Girs, G. F.; Dolenko, S. P.; Korgun, V. G.; Polyakov, G. A.; and Trinich, F. A., eds. *Demokraticheskaya respublika Afganistana* [Democratic Republic of Afghanistan]. Moscow: Nauka, 1981.

Attar, Ghafur. "Das Volk an der Macht." *Antiimperialistische Informationsbulletin* (Marburg, West Germany), no. 7/8 (July/August 1978): 42–49.

Background Briefs. London: United Kingdom Foreign and Commonwealth Office. (Ad hoc publications on matters of international interest; numerous issues on Afghanistan.)

Baddeley, John F. *The Russian Conquest of the Caucasus*. London: Longmans, Green and Company, 1908.

Bennigsen, Alexandre, and Quelquejay, Chantal. *Les Mouvements nationaux chez les Musulmans de Russie*. Paris: Mouton and Cie, 1960.

Bennigsen, Alexandre, and Wimbusch, S. Enders. *Muslim National Communism in the Soviet Union*. Chicago: University of Chicago Press, 1979.

Berner, Wolfgang. "Der Kampf um Kabul: Lehren und Perspektiven." In Heinrich Vogel, ed., *Die sowjetische Intervention in Afghanistan*. Baden Baden, West Germany: Nomos Verlagsgesellschaft, 1980, pp. 319–66.

Bittman, Ladislav. *The Deception Game*. New York: Ballantine Books, 1972.

Borcke, Astrid von. "Die Intervention in Afghanistan: Das Ende der sowjetischen Koexistenzpolitik?" *Berichte des Bundesinstituts fuer ostwissenschaftliche und internationale Studien*, no. 6 (1980).

Bradsher, Henry S. *Afghanistan and the Soviet Union*. Durham, N.C.: Duke University Press, 1983.

Burks, R. V. *The Dynamics of Communism in Eastern Europe*. Princeton, N. J.: Princeton University Press, 1961.

————. "Die nahende Kriese in der Sowjetunion," 3 pts. *Osteuropa* 33: 449–62, 555–68, and 705–23.

Carrère d'Encausse, Hélène. *L'Empire éclaté: La révolte des nations en U.R.S.S.*. Paris: Flammarion, 1978. Available in English as *Decline of an Empire: The Soviet Socialist Republics in Revolt*. Translated by Marin Sokolinsky and Henry A. La Farge. New York: Newsweek Books, 1979.

Chaliand, Gerard. *Rapport sur la résistance afghan*. Paris: Berger-Levrault, 1981.

Charters, David. "Resistance to Soviet Occupation of Afghanistan: Problems and Prospects." *Conflict Quarterly* 1, no. 1 (Summer 1980): 8–15.

Conquest, Robert. *The Great Terror: Stalin's Purges of the Thirties*. New York, Macmillan, 1968.

Critchlow, James. "Minarets and Marx." *Washington Quarterly*, Spring 1980, pp. 47–57.

Dupree, Louis. *Afghanistan*. Princeton, N.J.: Princeton University Press, 1978. (An insert, *Epilogue 1980*, is available for current printings.)

————. "Afghanistan Under the Khalq." *Problems of Communism*, July–August 1979, pp. 34–50.

————. American Universities Field Staff (AUFS) Reports, South Asia and Asia Series. Hanover, N.H.: AUFS. (From 1959 to 1980, Dupree was the AUFS referent for Afghanistan in this series of monographs.)

Dupree, Louis, and Albert, Linette, eds. *Afghanistan in the 1970s*. New York: Praeger, 1974.

Ege, Konrad. "Dans Kaboul aux prises avec ses rebelles." *Le Monde diplomatique* 354 (September 1983): 16–18.

Eudin, Xenia J., and North, Robert C. *Soviet Russia and the East, 1920–1927: A Documentary Survey*. Stanford: Stanford University Press, 1957.

Fischer, Louis. *The Soviets in World Affairs*. London: J. Cape, 1930.

Franck, Peter. *Afghanistan Between East and West*. Washington, D.C.: National Planning Association, 1960.

Fraser-Tytler, W. Kerr. *Afghanistan*. London: Oxford University Press, 1967.

Fredericks, Pierce G. *The Sepoy and the Cossack*. New York: World Publishing, 1971.

Garrity, Patrick J. "The Soviet Military Stake in Afghanistan, 1956–79." *RUSI: Journal of the Royal United Services Institute for Defence Studies* 125, no. 3 (September 1980): 31–36.

Gerasimova, A., and Girs, G. *Literatura Afganistana: Kratkiy ocherk* [The literature of Afghanistan: A brief essay]. Moscow: Izdatel'stvo vostochnoy literatury, 1963.

Golovin, Oleg. "Of the Friends and Enemies of Independent Revolutionary Afghanistan." *New Times*, no. 12 (March 1980): 7–9.

Grassmuck, G. L.; Adamec, L. W.; and Irwin, F. H., eds. *Afghanistan: Some New Approaches*. Ann Arbor: University of Michigan, Center for Near East and North African Studies, 1969.

Gregorian, Vartan. *The Emergence of Modern Afghanistan*. Stanford: Stanford University Press, 1969.

Halliday, Alfred. "The Revolution in Afghanistan." *New Left Review*, no. 112 (November–December 1978): 3–44.

Hammond, Thomas T. *Red Flag over Afghanistan: The Communist Coup, the Soviet Invasion, and the Consequences.* Boulder, Colo.: Westview Press, 1984.

Harrison, Selig S. "Dateline Afghanistan: Exit Through Finland?" *Foreign Policy*, no. 41 (Winter 1980–81): 163–87.

———. "Nightmare in Baluchistan." *Foreign Policy*, no. 32 (Fall 1978): 136–59.

Hussain, S. S.; Alvi, A. H.; and Rizvi, A. H. *Afghanistan Under Soviet Occupation.* Islamabad: World Affairs Publications, 1980.

Hyman, Anthony. *Afghanistan Under Soviet Domination.* London: Macmillan, 1982.

Ignatov, A. V. *Revolyutsiya, rozhdennaya v aprele* [The revolution born in April]. Moscow: Politicheskaya literatura, 1980.

Jäkel, Klaus. "Nur Mohammed Taraki." *Afghanistan Journal* 5, no. 3 (1978): 105–8.

Jewett, A. C. *An American Engineer in Afghanistan.* Edited by Marjorie Jewett Bell. Minneapolis: University of Minnesota Press, 1948.

Kazemzadeh, Firuz. "Afghanistan: The Imperial Dream." *New York Review of Books* 27, no. 2 (February 21, 1980): 10–14.

Khalilzad, Zalmay. *The Return of the Great Game.* Discussion Paper no. 88. Santa Monica, Calif.: California Seminar on International Security and Foreign Policy, September 1980.

———. "The Struggle for Afghanistan." *Survey* 25, no. 2 (Spring 1980): 189–216.

Klass, R. T. "The Great Game Revisited." *National Review*, October 26, 1979, pp. 1366–368.

Korgun, V. G. *Afganistan v 20-30-e gody XX v.* [Afghanistan in the twenties and thirties of the twentieth century]. Moscow: Nauka, 1979.

Krishnan, N. K. "Prospects of Democratic Advance in Afghanistan." *Party Life* (New Delhi), May 26, 1976, pp. 7–8.

Kunitz, Joshua. *Dawn over Samarkand: The Rebirth of Central Asia.* New York: Covici Friede, 1935.

Lifschulz, Lawrence. "L'Union sovietique peut-elle retirer ses troupes?" *Le Monde diplomatique* 354 (September 1983): 13–14.

———. "Un Atout pour Moscou: L'Irrédentisme du Baloutchistan." *Le Monde diplomatique* 354 (September 1983): 14–15.

Luttwak, Edward N. "After Afghanistan, What?" *Commentary* 69, no. 4 (April 1980): 40–49.

Male, Beverly. *Revolutionary Afghanistan.* New York: St. Martin's Press, 1982.

Manzar, H. M. *Red Clouds over Afghanistan.* Islamabad: Institute for Policy Studies, 1980.

Misra, K. P., ed. *Afghanistan Crisis.* New Delhi: Vikas Publishing, 1981.

Missen, François. *Le Syndrome de Kaboul.* Aix-en-Provence: Edisud, 1980.

Monks, Alfred L. *The Soviet Intervention in Afghanistan.* Washington, D.C.: American Enterprise Institute, 1981.

Nayar, Kuldip. *Report on Afghanistan.* New Delhi: Allied Publishing, 1981.

Negaran, Hannah [pseud.]. "The Afghan Coup of April 1978: Revolution and International Security." *Orbis* 23, no. 1 (Spring 1979): 93–113.

―――. "Afghanistan: A Marxist Regime in a Muslim Society." *Current History* 76 (1979): 172–74.

Newell, Nancy Peabody, and Newell, Richard S. *The Struggle for Afghanistan.* Ithaca, N.Y.: Cornell University Press, 1981.

Newell, Richard S. *The Politics of Afghanistan.* Ithaca, N.Y.: Cornell University Press, 1972.

Nollau, Guenther, and Wiehe, Hans Juergen. *Russia's South Flank.* New York: Praeger, 1963.

Noorani, A. G. "Afghanistan and the Rule of Law." *The Review* (New York: American Association for the International Commission of Jurists), no. 24 (June 1980): 37–52.

Nukhovich, E. *Vneshnyaya politika Afganistana* [Afghanistan's foreign policy]. Moscow: Institut mezhdunarodnykh otnosheniy, 1962.

Ochildiyev, D. Ya. *Obshchestvenno-politicheskaya mysl' Afganistana nakanune zavoyevaniya nezavisimosti* [Sociopolitical thought of Afghanistan on the eve of achieving independence]. Tashkent: Akademiya nauk uzbekskoy SSR, 1972.

On the Saur Revolution. Kabul: People's Democratic Party of Afghanistan in the Armed Forces of Afghanistan, Political Department, May 22, 1978.

Paul, Arthur. "Constraints on Afghanistan's Development and Prospects for Future Progress." Address to the Asia Society's Afghanistan Council, March 1973. New York: Asia Society, 1973.

Pennar, Jaan. *The USSR and the Arabs: The Ideological Dimension.* New York: Crane, Russak, 1973.

Phillips, James. "The Soviet Invasion of Afghanistan." *Backgrounder.* Washington, D.C.: Heritage Foundation, January 9, 1980.

Pikulin, M. T. *Razvitiye ekonomii i kultury Afganistana, 1955–60* [Development of the economy and culture of Afghanistan, 1955–1960]. Tashkent: Akademiya nauk uzbekskoy SSR, 1961.

Polyakov, Yu. A., and Chugunov, A. I. *Konets basmachestva* [The end of the Basmachi movement]. Moscow: Nauka, 1976.

Pope, Ronald R. "Afghanistan and the Influence of Public Opinion on Soviet Foreign Policy." *Asian Affairs*, July–August 1981: 346–52.

Poullada, Leon B. "Afghanistan and the United States: The Crucial Years." *Middle East Journal* 35, no. 2 (Spring 1981): 178–90.

———. "Afghanistan Searches for Unity." Library, University of Nebraska, Omaha, n.d. [late 1973?].

———. *Reform and Rebellion in Afghanistan, 1919–1929: King Amanullah's Failure to Modernize a Tribal Society*. Ithaca, N.Y.: Cornell University Press, 1973.

Ratnam, Perala. *Afghanistan's Uncertain Future*. New Delhi: Tulsi Publishing House, 1981.

Rees, David. "Afghanistan's Role in Soviet Strategy." *Conflict Studies*, no. 118 (May 1980).

Report of the Five Months' Performance of the D. R. A. Kabul: Afghanistan Publicity Bureau, October 1978.

Rideout, Christine F. "Authority Patterns and the Afghan Coup of 1973." *Middle East Journal* 29, no. 2 (Spring 1975): 165–78.

de Riencourt, Amaury. "Pakistan and India in the Shadow of Afghanistan." *Foreign Affairs* (Winter 1982–83): 416–37.

Rodinson, Maxime. *Marxism and the Muslim World*. Translated by Michael Pallis. London: Zed Press, 1979.

Rubinstein, Alvin Z. *Soviet Policy Toward Turkey, Iran, and Afghanistan*. New York: Praeger, 1982.

A Short Biography of Noor Mohammad Taraki. Kabul (?), August 23, 1978.

A Short Information About People's Democratic Party of Afghanistan. Kabul, 1978.

Shahrani, M. Nazif, and Canfield, Robert L., eds. *Revolutions and Rebellions in Afghanistan: Anthropological Perspectives*. Berkeley and Los Angeles: University of California Press, 1984.

Sidenko, Victor. "Two Years of the Afghan Revolution." *New Times*, no. 17 (May 1980): 18–25.

Sinha, Sri Prakash. *Afghanistan in Aufruhr*. Freiburg and Zurich, Switzerland: Hecht Verlag, 1980.

Smith, Harvey H. et al., eds. *Area Handbook for Afghanistan*, 4th ed. Washington, D.C.: Government Printing Office, 1973.

Smolar, Aleksander. "Afghanistan et Pologne." *Esprit* (January 1981): 91–95.

Stepanov, V. "Afghanistan on the Path of Revolutionary Change." *International Affairs* (Moscow) no. 5, 1984.

Taraki, Nur Mohammed. *Basic Lines of Revolutionary Duties of Government of Democratic Republic of Afghanistan.* Text of the radio address of May 9, 1978. Kabul, 1978.

————. *Report by Nur Mohammed Taraki, General Secretary of the PDPA CC, Presented to the Historical Plenum of the Central Committee of the People's Democratic Republic of Afghanistan Held on the Sixth of Qaus 1357* [November 28, 1978]. Kabul: People's Democratic Party of Afghanistan, Central Committee, Political Bureau, November 1978.

Tellinskii, L. B. *Sovetsko-afganskiye otnosheniya, 1919–1960* [Soviet-Afghan relations, 1919–1960]. Moscow: Sotsial'no-ekonomicheskaya literatura, 1964.

Tulenko, Thomas. "Two Invasions of Afghanistan." *History Today* 30 (June 1980): 7–12.

U.S. Congress. House. Committee on Foreign Affairs. *Soviet Violation of Helsinki Final Act: Invasion of Afghanistan; Hearings.* July 22, 1981. Washington, D.C.: Government Printing Office, 1981.

U.S. Department of State. Bureau of Public Affairs. *Afghanistan: 18 Months of Occupation.* Special Report no. 86, prepared by Eliza van Hollen. Washington, D.C., August 1981.

————. *Afghanistan: A Year of Occupation.* Special Report no. 79. Washington, D.C., February 1981.

————. *Afghanistan: Four Years of Occupation.* Special Report no. 112. Washington, D.C., December 1983.

————. *Afghanistan: Three Years of Occupation.* Special Report no. 106. Washington, D.C., December 1982.

————. *Soviet Dilemmas in Afghanistan.* Special Report no. 72. Washington, D.C., June 1980.

————. Special Assignments Staff, Office of Security. *Summary of Report of Investigation: The Kidnapping and Death of Ambassador Adolph Dubs, February 14, 1979, Kabul, Afghanistan.* Washington, D.C., n.d. (presumably late 1979).

————. U.S. Embassy, Kabul. "The Afghan Left." Airgram A-33, May 22, 1973.

————. "The 'Left' in Afghanistan." Airgram A-24, April 29, 1975.

Valenta, Jiri. "From Prague to Kabul: The Soviet Style of Invasion." *International Security* (Harvard University Center for Science and International Affairs), no. 630 (Fall 1980): 114–41.

Vinogradov, V. M. et al., eds. *Sovetsko-afganskiye otnosheniya, 1919–1969* [Soviet-Afghan relations, 1919–1969]. Moscow: Politizdat, 1971.

Volkov, Y.; Gevorkyan, K.; Mikhailenko, M.; Polonsky, P.; and Svetozarov, A., comps. *The Truth About Afghanistan: Documents, Facts, Eyewitness Reports*. Moscow: Novosti Press Agency Publishing House, 1980.

Warhurst, Geoffrey. "Afghanistan: A Dissenting Appraisal." *RUSI: Journal of the Royal United Services Institute for Defense Studies*, no. 125 (September 1980): 26–29.

Weinland, Robert G. *An (The?) Explanation of the Soviet Invasion of Afghanistan*. Professional Paper 309. Washington, D.C.: Center for Naval Analysis, May 1981.

Wiegandt, Winfried F. *Afghanistan: Nicht aus heiterem Himmel*. Zurich: Orell Fuessli Verlag, 1980.

"World Communist Solidarity with the Afghan Revolution." *New Times*, no. 3 (January 1980): 8–10.

Zeary, Saleh M. "Afghanistan: The Beginning of a New Era." *The World Marxist Review* 22, no. 1 (January 1979): 73–78.

Index